Hitler's Storm Troopers
A History of the SA

Hitler's Storm Troopers
A History of the SA

The Memoirs of Wilfred von Oven

Wilfred von Oven

Introduction by
Eleanor Hancock

Translated by
Geoffrey Brooks

Frontline Books
London

Hitler's Storm Troopers: A History of the SA
This edition published in 2010 by Frontline Books,
an imprint of Pen & Sword Books Ltd,
47 Church Street, Barnsley, S. Yorkshire, S70 2AS
www.frontline-books.com

Copyright © Wilfred von Oven, 1998
Translation © Pen & Sword Books Limited, 2010
This edition © Pen & Sword Books Limited, 2010
Introduction © Eleanor Hancock, 2010

ISBN: 978-1-84832-576-0

PUBLISHING HISTORY
This memoir was published originally in German by Arndt-Verlag under the
title *Mit ruhig festem Schritt: Aus der Geschichte der SA* (*With Firm and
Measured Steps: The Autobiography of an SA Man*) in 1998. It was translated
into Spanish – *Con paso firme y pausado* – by Galland Books in 2008.
This is the first English-language edition, and includes an introduction
by Eleanor Hancock.

Images for plates 1–7 courtesy of Galland Books.

CIP data records for this title are available
from the British Library

For more information on our books, please visit
www.frontline-books.com, email info@frontline-books.com
or write to us at the above address.

Printed in Great Britain by MPG Books Limited

Typeset in 11.3/15.3 point Sabon

Contents

Illustrations

Introduction

In January 1933 the National Socialist German Workers' Party (the NSDAP or Nazis) came to power in Germany. The resulting dictatorship unleashed a war and genocides that lastingly altered the world. The generation who experienced this period of history as adults are now extremely old and passing from the scene. This makes their surviving eyewitness accounts even more valuable to all who seek to understand the Nazi regime.

Wilfried (or Wilfred) von Oven was a Nazi 'outsider' whose long life gave him the opportunity to be active in neo-Nazi affairs, to set out his own memories of the period and to advance his own positive interpretations of the Third Reich. Oven was born in Bolivia in 1912 but returned to Germany as a young child. Oven supported National Socialism but was often at a distance from it. He was only a member of the party and the Nazi storm troopers for a year before resigning in the aftermath of a revolt in the Berlin Sturmabteilung or SA (the Stennes revolt). Later, however, he reconciled himself with the Nazi regime, working as a reporter in the Spanish Civil War and then as a Propaganda Ministry war correspondent. From 1943 to 1945 he was the personal press adjutant of Propaganda Minister Joseph Goebbels. Soon after the war, Oven published a diary of his time with Goebbels, *Finale Furioso*. While this is a valuable source for the last stages of the war, it must be used with caution as sections of it were clearly revised and edited after the war.

In the 1950s Oven settled in Argentina where he lived for the rest of his life. In the 1950s he was briefly the Latin American correspondent for the German news weekly *Der Spiegel*. Oven was active in neo-Nazi circles until his death. He died in Argentina on 14 June 2008 aged 96.[*]

In 1998 Oven published this combined history and memoir of the SA – *Mit ruhig festem Schritt – Aus der Geschichte der SA*, which Frontline Books is publishing here for the first time in English. In the Nazi rise to power a key role was played by the Nazi storm troopers, the SA. The SA was a paramilitary organization designed for defence of Nazi Party meetings and attacks on its political opponents. It formed the workforce for the unceasing Nazi political activity in the lead-up to the takeover of power in 1933. In 1933–4 the SA provided the violence and the threat of violence necessary for the party to take over and consolidate power. Despite its pivotal role until 1934, when it was purged and rendered politically powerless, the SA has been surprisingly under-studied by historians. Serious academic studies have only begun to appear since the 1980s.[†]

---

[*] Jörg Schule, 'NS: Wilfried von Oven Der Tod des Nazis', sueddeutsche.de, 7 October 2008, www.sueddeutsche.de/politik/231/313139/text/print.html, accessed 21 November 2009.

[†] Thomas Balistier, *Gewalt und Ordnung: Kalkül und Faszination der SA* (Verlag Westfälisches Dampfboot, Münster, 1989); Richard Bessel, *Political Violence and the Rise of Nazism: The Stormtroopers in Eastern Germany 1925–1934* (Yale University Press, London, 1984); Bruce Campbell, *The SA Generals and the Rise of Nazism* (University Press of Kentucky, Lexington, Ky., 1998); Conan Fischer, *Stormtroopers: A Social, Economic and Ideological Analysis, 1929–35* (George Allen and Unwin, London, 1983); Thomas D. Grant, *Stormtroopers and Crisis in the Nazi Movement: Activism, ideology and dissolution* (Routledge, London, 2004); Mathilde Jamin, *Zwischen den Klassen: zur Sozialstruktur der SA-Führerschaft* (Peter Hammer Verlag, Wuppertal, 1984); Peter Longerich, *Die braunen Bataillonen: Geschichte der SA* (Verlag C. H. Beck, Munich, 1989); Peter H. Merkl, *Making of a*

Oven's Nazism was inextricably linked with the career of Joseph Goebbels, not only as Propaganda Minister during the war but also as Nazi Party regional leader (*Gauleiter*) of Berlin in the early 1930s. Oven's experience was of the SA in Berlin, the capital of Germany. The Berlin SA was generally more provocative, violent and radical than the SA in many other areas of Germany. This difference arose in part because 'Red' Berlin was also a centre of Communist strength in the Weimar Republic, the democratic regime that preceded Nazi Germany. The techniques of the Berlin SA were developed with Goebbels's support and were used to gain publicity for the party. A series of SA men who were killed by their political opponents, most notably Horst Wessel, became seen as 'martyrs' for National Socialism as a result of Goebbels's staging of their funerals.

The Berlin SA was hard for the party to control. In summer 1930 and again in spring 1931 the Berlin SA led by Gruppen-führer Walther Stennes revolted against the party leadership. These revolts were fuelled both by policy disagreements – Stennes opposed the legal path to power that the party was pursuing – and by economic grievances on the part of the SA.* It was the second of these revolts that saw Oven also leave the party and SA.

Even though the Berlin SA was not always typical of the SA in general, because of its prominence and because of its role in pre-1933 Nazi propaganda, it was the Berlin SA that created the popular image of these 'party soldiers' both at the time and

Stormtrooper (Princeton University Press, Princeton, N.J., 1980); Sven Reichardt, *Faschistische Kampfbünde: Gewalt und Gemein-schaft im italienischen Squadrismus und in der deutschen SA* (Böhlau Verlag, Cologne, 2002); Eric G. Reiche, *The Development of the SA in Nürnberg, 1922–1934* (Cambridge University Press, Cambridge, 1986).

* Bernhard Sauer, 'Goebbels "Rabauken" Zur Geschichte der SA in Berlin-Brandenburg', in *Geschichte und Gegenwart. Jahrbuch des Landesarchivs Berlin 2006*, www.bernhard-sauer-historiker.de, downloaded 21 November 2009.

afterwards. Oven's study in this book combines both a report of his own time in the SA together with his history of the SA. The book is most valuable when it recounts Oven's own experiences in the SA, his own views at the time and his personal encounters with Goebbels. It is also important as a frank presentation of what motivated Nazi supporters and how they saw their experiences. It is also a valuable source for the divergences of opinion on politics and tactics inside the SA, which made it among the most turbulent of all Nazi organizations.

This history is an unapologetic defence of the SA against post-war revelations and historical interpretations. As such, it must be read with caution and with the awareness that it presents a strongly pro-SA point of view. The individual details Oven sets out are not always accurate, and the book should be understood as a counter to a German study of the SA that appeared just before his book was published, Peter Longerich's *Die braunen Bataillonen*. These aims though make the book interesting as an example of postwar neo-Nazi self-understandings. Oven shocked British film maker Laurence Rees by describing his experience of Nazi rule as paradise.* Like all Oven's postwar writing, this study allows us to understand how and why Oven and others like him persisted in such attitudes and tried to spread them.

This book is a valuable source and well worth reading, but it must be read with caution and an awareness of its author's political agenda.

Eleanor Hancock
University College,
University of
New South Wales

* Richard Jinman, 'Hearts of darkness', *Sydney Morning Herald*, 29 September 2005, www.smh.com.au/news/tv-radio/hearts of darkness/2005/09/24/1126982268912.html, accessed 17 Jan. 2010.

Chapter 1

Why Brown?

Hitler hated the colour brown. Not many of us who made up the 'brown battalions' liked it either. I could understand the continuing prohibition on the wearing of paramilitary uniforms dictated by the Weimar government, and in the end I never wore uniform during all the time I was in the SA. There were a few hundred thousand of us, and we went about dressed almost like vagrants. Our attire bore few similarities to the outfits sported by the SA at the time of its creation in Munich. All the same we felt as comfortable as the first fighters had been in their field-grey country jackets and Austrian ski hats, designed by Hitler himself.

We young SA men of the epoch of struggle in Berlin wore naval caps with shiny peaks and cloth or leather face-masks. To go with this we had uniform footwear of motorcycle boots with shiny heels and a leather buckle. All else was down to personal taste.

The only item we had in common with the original Munich SA, and the SA of the Third Reich, was the red armband with black swastika emblazoned on a white circle which we wore on the left upper arm. This armband was popular not for its most ancient symbol of the Aryan race but for the black-white-red mixture of colours. But brown? Why should it be brown [*braun* in German]? Was it a play on words by the Führer, who was born at Braunau? Was there some mysterious prophetic connection with Eva Braun, his companion-to-be and future wife?

Our political adversaries had the true reason of course. The Spartans of Greece, they said, wore red shirts so that it was difficult to see the blood. Our shirts on the other hand, would hide the evidence of another kind of bodily product resulting from fear. A cynical joke did the rounds. The 'hero', a fictional character by the name of Bonifacio Kiesewetter, had attended the Party Congress, placing himself amongst the faithful thousands below the masses of waving Hitler flags. At the end of the great oration all shouted '*Sieg Heil!*' except Bonifacio who yelled 'Shit!' and gave great offence. It was not his only insolent observation. Under interrogation he explained that with so much brown around his senses had become confused. Unlike Bonifacio, the brown shirts did not make us dizzy. We simply did not like the colour and neither did Hitler.

The National Socialist Movement had not chosen it. The most recent scientific investigation puts the origins of the colour beyond any doubt. Peter Longerich, staff member at the Institute of Contemporary History in Munich, a body acting in the service of re-educating the German people, and which never in its existence ever saw an SA man in the flesh, draws attention in his book[*] to a resolution agreed during the Party conference of 17/18 May 1924 (at present to be found in the Munich Government archive). Here we find laid down the new directives for the SA, and mention of some 'Lettow' shirts, which for Longerich can only be those shirts worn by Imperial German troops under General von Lettow-Vorbeck in Germany's African colonies during the Great War and which were to be the 'model' for the Nazis.

The reality is rather more prosaic. Göring had convened the SA chiefs in exile to a meeting in Salzburg where, amongst other matters, the question of dress was discussed, and the opportunity taken to make a decision. Göring had an adjutant by the name of Gerhard Rossbach. During the famous march to

[*] Peter Longerich, *Die braunen Bataillonen*, Beck, Munich, 1989.

the Feldherrnhalle on 9 November 1923, where Hitler failed in his attempt to topple the Communist government of Munich, and sixteen Party men were shot down, Rossbach had led a column of volunteers. He happened to know of a large stock of shirts in store in Austria which had been intended for General von Lettow-Vorbeck's troops in Africa. Before they could be shipped out the war had ended. Rossbach arranged their purchase through a friend with whom he had fought against the French in the Ruhr, and against the Poles in Upper Silesia in a Freikorps at the beginning of the 1920s. This friend, Edmund Heines, was a Munich businessman who had joined the SA in 1922. Through the firm Sportversand Schill (a distributor of sporting goods) owned by Heines, Rossbach acquired the shirts for the SA.

When preparations were begun to reorganize the SA in May 1924 under the guidance of General Ludendorff, with the designation 'Circle of Popular Defence', Rossbach issued the first directive on the subject of the uniform: brown shirt ('Lettow' type), cap ('Hitler' type), field-grey, green or brown breeches, boots or boots with high-laced gaiters. This was how Röhm envisaged his 'Vanguard Group' similar to the SA but independent of it and with a growing membership which eventually reached 30,000.[*]

Upon his release from Landsberg Prison, Hitler saw that the status and aims of the new SA could not accommodate Röhm's corps and they would have to separate. Since the elitist SS troop was not large enough for Hitler's propaganda purposes, he named as Supreme SA Chief the Gauleiter of Westphalia, Franz Pfeffer von Salomon, and dissolved Röhm's 'Vanguard Group'. Salomon took up his post on 1 November 1924.

Two years later, on 14 November 1926, he issued instructions for uniform wear: brown shirt with tie and cap, short brown trousers, a belt over the right shoulder and a belt for the

[*] Heinz Höhne, *Mordsache Röhm*, Rheinbek, 1984.

trousers. In addition at this time a field-grey jacket was permitted to be worn over the shirt. This was a concession to the Great War combatants, such as Röhm and his chief of staff Rossbach, who had formed the nucleus of the SA. Contrary to what the occupying forces ordered after the Second World War, soldiers returning from the fronts at the end of the First World War had retained their dress worn on the field of honour, while even the young men of the SA who had not had a baptism of fire wore field-grey.

The war against the victorious Allies had ended (although they soon invaded the Ruhr, the richest coal-mining region in Europe), but the struggle went on against Bolshevism, the 'November criminals', the Socialists ('Sozis') and the Jews, these last being held responsible for Germany's present sorry plight, the situation having degenerated despite Germany's forces being undefeated on the fronts. The definitive introduction of the brown uniform for the SA took place on 20 August 1929 on the instructions of Pfeffer von Salomon, as has been reliably confirmed by retired US Lieutenant Colonel John R. Angolia in his exhaustive study of Nazi Party and SA uniforms.*

The 'inventor' – probably unintentional – of the brown shirt worn by millions, Gerhard Rossbach, was one of those typical soldierly figures moulded within German youth by the Great War. Frustrated more by the treason of the 'November criminals' than by the deceit of President Wilson's '14 Points for Peace', this young lieutenant of Artillery Regiment 175 had an indomitable desire for action. Scarcely had the guns fallen silent in November 1918 than he created Freikorps *Rossbach* in which he hurled himself into the fray, taking it upon himself to begin a quest to reverse the territorial transgressions by Poland in the German east.

In January 1919 he liberated the town of Kulm in West Prussia, occupied by the Poles. In recognition of this service, the

* John R. Angolia, *Cloth Insignia of the NSDAP and SA*, San José, California, 1985.

Weimar government accepted his Freikorps into the Reichswehr, the regular Army cut down to size by the victors to a
miserable maximum 100,000 men. Rossbach and his followers
did not last long as soldiers, however. In 1920 when the
bemonocled General Hans von Seeckt was appointed Chief of
the Army General Staff and given the task of reorganization,
there was no longer a place in the ranks of the Weimar Republic
Army for the likes of Rossbach: 'The combatants were obliged
to give up their places to the military', French author
Dominique Venner stated in his history of the Freikorps.[*]

The Freikorps, Seeckt declared, had the character of the
seventeenth-century *Landsknecht*, a kind of suicide vanguard
ahead of the infantry. These people were inappropriate material
from which to form a large part of a regular Army. Basically he
was not far wrong, taking into account the terms of reference
the government had given him. On the other hand he was
sufficiently objective to recognize that what motivated the
Freikorps was a burning sense of injustice and their displeasure
at the performance of the wartime Army. They would resent its
members in the Reichswehr and turn them into bitter enemies,
as they would the fledgling German democracy and Seeckt
himself. All the same Seeckt took the risk. His decision was
wrong and had serious consequences. The vengeful spirit
awoken by the dictates of Versailles could not accept the
measures adopted and the Freikorps would have their revenge.
They found their spot in Hitler's movement and finally brought
about the downfall of the Weimar Republic.

Arnolt Bronnen, who was no nationalist and even less a
Nazi, defined Gerhard Rossbach in an enthusiastic biography[†]
of this so-typical figure from that confused epoch:

'He considered it his mission to reunite the men and transform them into soldiers, while looking for trouble, drinking,
making disturbances, breaking windows, smashing everything

[*] Dominique Venner, *Baltikum*, Paris, 1974.
[†] Arnolt Bronnen, *Rossbach*, Berlin 1930.

in reach to smithereens, living without scruples and being hard without compassion.' It would be difficult to find parallels in any of the points of the National Socialist Party programme that Hitler was in the process of drawing up together with Anton Drexler at the same time. However, Rossbach wanted something similar to what Hitler wanted, although put a different, far more drastic way: 'We have to open the sore on the sick national body and drain it until the blood comes out. Allow it to run for the time it needs to get it clean.' This they did.

What Rossbach and Röhm wanted, just like Heines and Heidebreck, Helldorf, Schneidhuber and many others of the Freikorps, was to be realized in the SA. In the beginning there was scarcely a group of SA men not led by some Freikorps officer. It was a logical evolution. Soldiers serving with the Mortar Company of 19th Infantry Regiment stationed at Munich formed the first team set up to provide protection at Party meetings for the former Reichswehr political instructor and blossoming popular leader, Adolf Hitler. The team was designated Saalschutz-Abteilung SA. The men were sent as civilians after regular duty in barracks. There was a close affinity between these soldiers and the orator Hitler, for after all he had been one of them. What he expressed concerned them; what he was saying they felt deeply.

Soon came replacements in the form of volunteers of whom there was no shortage. In time, the Hitler movement distanced itself from its military roots, although most who belonged, and above all its leader, never lost contact with them. It is here that one must search to find the origins of many of the internal conflicts within the SA.

The relationship between Rossbach and Lettow-Vorbeck developed at the time of Kapp's failed coup d'état in March 1920. The commanding officer of the Imperial troops who had so successfully defended the German colonies in East Africa (modern Tanzania) against British, Portuguese and Belgian forces fifteen times more numerous, was transferred as a general into the Reichswehr after the Great War. During the summer of 1919 he suppressed the attempted Communist coup in Hamburg, where the idea had been to establish a Soviet republic along the lines of the model established briefly in Bavaria.

Allied with General Walter von Lüttwitz, Supreme Commander of the Reichswehr, he lent his support to the preparations for the coup being organized in March 1920 by the Director General for the Environment, Wolfgang Kapp, a native of Königsberg. Kapp failed in his attempt. Lettow-Vorbeck, Lüttwitz and other senior officers were of the opinion that the government had to be overthrown using the most ruthless measures if necessary. In this respect Lettow-Vorbeck could draw on his own experiences at Hamburg, as could Lüttwitz from his putting down of the Communist Spartacist rising in Berlin in early 1919, and also General Ernst von Oven* who had helped overthrow the Red revolutionary council in Munich. The military leaders were of the opinion that there should be no difficulty. When differences of opinion emerged later, these related only to the political aspect.

At odds with the Lüttwitz–Lettow combination were General Maercker, General Ernst von Oven and their followers, who warned their companions not to meddle in the sticky field of politics or, even worse, toy with the idea of establishing a military dictatorship. All were united as to the aim, however, which was to save Germany from Bolshevism. Only in their methodology was there a lack of concord.

Kapp's coup failed precisely for these internal differences and not for a supposed loyalty of the Socialist bureaucracy towards its democratic government or a general strike as is purported to be the case in modern publications and scholarly texts.[†]

* Uncle of the author.
[†] General Lüttwitz seized Berlin on 13 March 1920. Chancellor Ebert withdrew to Dresden with his government. Kapp received support from General Ludendorff, but the officer corps (*cont. on p. 20*)

The coup leaders knew how to hit at the masses stirred up by professional Communist agitators and following orders received from Socialist Minister Noske. They were also successful on another occasion when the Communists attempted to topple the government as they had tried to do in November 1918. In these military moves, Leutnant Gerhard Rossbach played an important role. As mentioned previously, Freikorps *Rossbach* had been disbanded by the Berlin government. Rossbach kept his men together with the help of Hauptmann Waldemar Pabst, Chief of the Cavalry Staff, who had been involved in putting down the Spartacist revolt of January 1919 and was helping to organize a National Alliance in support of Kapp. A start was made by putting Rossbach and his men on the Reichswehr payroll. Later industrialists became interested in Kapp's success.

On 16 March 1920 the Communists believed that the moment had come to stage their own coup. As Lettow-Vorbeck had predicted they declared a political general strike in the provinces of Mecklenburg and Pomerania and organized the working classes into Red militia. Freikorps *Rossbach* intervened. In a lightning action he broke up the workers' in-surrection and tried the ringleaders on the spot. Three were executed immediately by firing squad. This put paid to the Communist coup. Rossbach and his men stood trial at Stettin for the incident in 1928, but the case was thrown out.

Lettow-Vorbeck had told Rossbach about the brown shirts which had been almost forgotten in store in Austria. Who could have forseen that those garments destined for another continent would be converted into a symbol of a political movement still vituperated three generations later? They were part and parcel of our national destiny whether or not we wore them. Whoever like myself does not believe that the history of our German people is simply a chain of fortuitous happenings, but rather is

(*cont. from p. 19*) stood back and remained impartial. This support was essential for the coup. On 17 March Kapp and Lüttwitz were forced to flee.

convinced that it is a logical consequence of interlinked, interdependent events forming the national destiny, will see that the patronage of Lettow-Vorbeck in providing the SA with its uniform has a profound meaning. Contemporary historians know something of our history but the detail that General von Lettow-Vorbeck was the patron of the brown shirt has escaped them.

Beyond any doubt the general would have joined our ranks had he been born a generation later, but when the Great War broke out he was already 44 years of age, twenty-five years of which he had spent in the service of the Imperial Army. He had won his first decorations at the turn of the century in helping to put down the Boxer Rebellion (1898–1900), an attempt to oust the foreign occupiers and Christians from China.* It was there where the British, no mean colonizers themselves, opted 'as gentlemen' to let the Germans 'bat first', thereby coining the phrase 'Germans to the front'.

A few years on and Lettow-Vorbeck applied the experience gained in China to the colonial war in southern Africa. The Bantus, coming from Central Africa, had invaded German colonial territory† causing serious losses in men and materials. In 1904 Berlin ordered Lettow-Vorbeck to repulse the invasion. He finally succeeded in 1907 at the Battle of Waterberg. Before the Great War began, Lettow-Vorbeck was appointed to command the troops defending German East Africa. These amounted to 216 German officers and NCOs and 2,540 black natives recruited as volunteers.

The British considered that this ridiculous little army would be easy to overwhelm with their contingent of 8,000 well-trained and equipped Sikhs which they disembarked at Tanga in modern Tanzania. The British were mistaken and their force

* Imperial Germany had a colonial enclave and naval base on the Chinese coast at Tsingtao (modern Qingdao) on the Shangdong Peninsula.
† Of modern Namibia.

was ejected after bloody fighting during November 1914. An American magazine referred to the 'total and embarrassing defeat of the British force'.* The British and their Empire troops were never able to overcome this 'Defensive Group', created from nothing and poorly armed, even when they sent in an army of 250,000 men with intact logistics. On 12 November 1918, when the Kaiser was already in exile in Holland after the proclamation of the Republic and the signing of the Armistice, Lettow-Vorbeck fought his last battle in Africa and laid down his arms when Berlin signalled him to.

In 1953, at the age of 83, the indomitable Lettow-Vorbeck travelled to Tanganyika, as it was then known, to be chaired on his arrival on the shoulders of his former native soldiers. Eleven years later in 1964 he returned to East Africa for the last time having convinced the West German government to settle its former colonial soldiers' claim for arrears of back-pay. He died the same year. His reception in Valhalla† must have been glorious. My old SA comrades there will certainly have nothing to be ashamed of in having worn the Lettow-Vorbeck brown shirt.

---

* *Instauration*, edition of December 1996.
† In Germanic mythology the hall of dead warriors who live on under Wotan awaiting the final battle of Ragnarok. Oven told writer Uki Goñi, *The Real Odessa*, Granta Books, 2003, pp. 322–3, that he remained a Nazi pagan.

CHAPTER 2

No Fun in the Pleasure Park

My admittedly quite pallid career in the ranks of the SA of Adolf Hitler's Nazi Party began on 1 May 1931. This unimportant detail may be verified in the Party's Central Archive, still carefully preserved in the German Federal Republic. Exactly one year later, on 1 May 1932, my career was truncated.

My joining the Nazi Party is punctiliously registered and so too my resignation from both institutions. I repeat: my resignation! To more than one opponent of the ideology, handing in one's notice would seem impossible, yet the truth is that this resignation never prejudiced my political or professional future at any time. Four days later I celebrated my twentieth birthday.

My entry into the Party and SA required something to 'push me into it' and I put this phrase in inverted commas because in effect it was a blow to the head which set it in train. It all began at the Berlin Lustgarten. In its day it had been conceived as a place of relaxation and pleasure for the inhabitants of the Prussian Royal Palace. It was built in the fifteenth century and renovated by the famous architect and sculptor Andreas Schlüter between 1697 and 1704. The Western Allies enjoyed destroying it at the end of World War II and their Bolshevist comrades-in-arms razed the ruins to the ground.

In my service as an SA man there was little hope of relaxation and tranquillity. Those beautiful gardens in the very heart of the German Reich had been transformed into circus arenas for the major political leaders of the Weimar Republic. Whilst its orators and politicians weighed their words for impact, the loyal masses tested the weight of their fists for the same purpose. Rally succeeded rally. From the extreme Left to the extreme Right, combatants squared up to each other. The police called upon ever larger contingents to prevent bloody rioting.

The Reich Chancellor at that time was Catholic trade unionist Heinrich Brüning (1885–1970) of the Centre Party, who achieved a doubtful fame with his rule by emergency decree. These decrees were given the nod by the respectable and respected Reich President von Hindenburg, and were used to help the government govern. A decree signed on 18 March 1931 aimed to 'curb political excesses', and I was to be one of its first victims. It came about thus:

My father, a loyal German resident abroad (Bolivia, in whose capital La Paz I was born in 1912) had returned to Germany with his family a little before the First World War. In June 1917 he fell in Flanders. My mother managed to keep her four small children fed for the remainder of the war and through the Allied food blockade with followed it (70,000 persons starved to death during this peacetime action, the majority children and the weak). Her meagre pension as a war-widow was hardly enough to make ends meet. From infancy we knew utter poverty and hunger. My brother and I formed part of the pitiable army of six million Germans for whom the state could find no work, much less pay them dole. National Socialism appeared to us to offer the best alternative in that intolerable situation especially since the social factor of its ideology harmonized with the deep-rooted Prussian military traditions of our family. My brother was one of those millions of electors who collaborated to produce that spectacular result achieved by the Nazi Party at a stroke on 14 September 1930. It advanced all of a sudden to being the second largest group in the Reichstag with ninety-five seats. This singular success motivated my brother and countless other citizens to join the political party which had achieved this meteoric rise.

By reason of my age I was not yet enfranchized – a voter had to be 21. Accordingly I was a simple sympathizer with the Nazis. The activists classified us as 'lapdogs'. Our badge was the Wolfsangel rune, a Germanic symbol used much later as the emblem of the National Socialist Jungvolk, formed of children aged from 10 to 14 (the under-tens could not enter the Hitler juvenile organization: National Socialist philosophy rigorously defended the principle that children should be brought up within the family without state interference or the hindrances of religious influences). Whoever wore the badge proclaimed his political orientation, but it did not also signify affiliation to a political party or allied organization.

The Stahlhelm (league of former front-line combatants) called a massive demonstration in the Lustgarten (Berlin's 'Park of Peace'). I wore the Wolfsangel in the lapel of my jacket. The 'Parties of the System', as we called all the political parties which dirtied their fingers supporting the corrupt Weimar administration, also arranged a demonstration for the same place and time. It looked very interesting. Without doubt there would be confrontations. The political leaders were very curious to see how their recent emergency decree aimed at suppressing political violence would work. I would soon see for myself at first hand.

The estimates of people attending varied considerably, as is customary in these events. The police talked of 'tens of thousands', others mentioned a hundred thousand. I have no idea how many people actually were there, but what I do know is that amongst that crush was a tall, thin youth dressed in civilian clothes and wearing a Wolfsangel rune in the lapel of his jacket. The badge brought me little luck when I fell in amongst the Reds. I was lifted out from the midst of them almost by the

ears by an SA man who ordered me to 'Clear off, boy!' With a
jerk of the head he indicated where the 'commune' was, the
name given by the SA men to Communist Party members, and
particularly the members of the Rot-Front Brigade (League of
Red Front Fighters).

Quite unintentionally I had drifted to the imaginary line
separating the rival blocks of Red and Brown paramilitaries.
Unlike myself, the police knew the two sides very well. They
also knew that the fighting always began on the imaginary line.
Armed with their emergency edict, the police were ready to
intervene using maximum force if the situation required. The
instrument they used in these emergencies was the hard-rubber
truncheon, which hung loose from the belt, and they were very
free with it. The Vice-President of Police, Bernard Weiss (given
the lyrical nickname Isidore Weiss by Goebbels) had told his
officers they could use the baton without regard to the injuries
they might inflict.

Never will I forget the spectacle I witnessed that day. We
were squashed together shoulder to shoulder on a sandy quad-
rangle of a few hundred square metres to one side of the
Lustgarten. Before us rose the imposing cathedral built by
Kaiser Wilhelm II. The majestic outside staircases were tinged
the green of spring by the uniforms of numerous squadrons of
police who crowded them. Poised to descend, they seemed to
be literally praying for something to happen within the human
mass below their feet. The slightest indication would be enough
to set in motion those gendarmes with their hard rubber
coshes.

For the time being all one heard from the opposing groups
was a chorus of insults, often culminating in mutual challenges
to 'put 'em up!' And suddenly came the spark which started it.
I do not know exactly where on that accursed invisible line
separating the two enemy blocs it began. I was on the line
because I had not yet managed to struggle through to safety as

ordered by the SA man. I was in the very eye of the tornado! And now I saw the hordes of police moving in like the making tide ...

It was a nightmare. I remember feeling a sudden terrible pain over my whole body caused by a police truncheon striking me violently in the nape of the neck. I staggered like a drunk. A gendarme caught me, and his steely hands extricated me half unconscious from the midst of the mob. I was brought to the 'Alex', the police station on the Alexander Platz. I was neither the first nor the last: the place gradually filled with fighters from both sides. It was my first visit to this inhospitable place. Much later, when I was an SA militant, I had the opportunity to enter this building involuntarily on a number of occasions. Generally we would be allowed to go after leaving our personal details. I returned home, which was located on the outskirts of Berlin, seized by the most vengeful emotions. I related nothing of the events to my mother or brothers. I felt a mixture of pain, disillusion, rage, irritation: a sea of emotions. I took the Wolfs-angel rune from my jacket in my fury. To that emblem I owed my place on the dividing line between the two opposing forces; I owed it the beating I had received. Now I had had enough. I vowed to exchange it for the red armband with the black swastika on a white disc, and the Nazi Party badge. It was such a minor thing which made me hard. I would not have gone ahead otherwise before reaching the age of majority. The next day I presented myself to the local Party HQ where I filled in an application form for the Nazi Party and the SA. The date they bore was 1 May 1931. On 4 May 1931 I completed my nineteenth year.

The man in charge of that modest little office was dressed in 'pirate' clothes as I was – the wearing of uniform was banned. He spoke with the Berlin accent. When I handed him the application forms he gave me a sceptical look and said, 'Your name is Wilfred von Oven?' When I agreed that it was he added, 'So you are of the nobility?' I nodded once more. 'Just like Prinz Auwi.' Here I had to correct him. 'Auwi' (August Wilhelm) was the son of the former Kaiser Wilhelm II, now living in exile in Holland. He was of a different breed to us, who were of the lower aristocracy. 'But Auwi is terrific,' my new SA comrade exclaimed. He had heard him speak at a Party meeting. 'He spoke like one of us. He is no idiot.'

In this I had to admit he was right. Auwi was no man's fool, although my future chief, Dr Joseph Goebbels, said of him in his personal diary that he was 'a very decent person but at times rather senile' (entry of 5 August 1929 after having met him at Nuremberg during the Party rally). For my part I think that Goebbels's judgment was inaccurate because Prinz August Wilhelm was 42 and Goebbels ten years his junior. Personal witnesses who knew him better described him as 'reserved'. Undoubtedly he was an introvert. He sketched and wrote poems. He had his own firm ideas about Germany's disastrous postwar economic situation. His opinions were much closer to ours than were those of his family, particularly his father the former Kaiser and his brothers. For that reason he had sought contact with NSDAP leaders.

Goebbels related in the diary entry mentioned previously that Prinz Auwi gave the impression of being rather withdrawn. 'Without beating about the bush I told him what I thought and he didn't take it the wrong way' he wrote, and he continued by asking himself, 'Can one make something out of him?' Certainly one could. A few months after that conversation with Goebbels, the prince, who in 1907 had obtained a doctorate in political science and administration at the University of Strassburg (then still German) and who was moreover a colonel and adviser to the Prussian government, joined the NSDAP. Hitler considered this to be so important that he gave him a very low membership number, 24, reserved for special cases. In 1933 Auwi, also an SA-man, was awarded the Party badge in gold, an honour so high that few military men could boast of it. Later he became a Reichstag deputy.

A little before the Second World War began, on 30 June 1939, he obtained the highest rank in the SA, Obergruppenführer, equivalent to an Army general. In 1945 he was arrested by the Allies and sentenced to two years six months forced labour, had his properties confiscated and was banned from exercising his profession as an administrator. Later the sentence of forced labour was commuted. He died on 25 March 1949 at the age of 62. Goebbels, who wrote frequently about the Hohenzollern prince in those parts of his diaries which have come down to us, called him 'a poor devil' in the entry for 17 December 1936, and to tell the truth, that affiliate of ancient lineage was one long before the victors and the re-educators of the German people brainwashed him. Goebbels completed the entry with the observation, 'he suffers amongst the other Hohenzollerns'.*

My future chief did not make so many references to the former Kaiser Wilhelm II (1859–1941), who in 1918 fled from the Marxist insurrectionists to Holland from where he could observe the fabulous rise of the Third Reich. Unlike his father and grandfather, his grandson Prinz Louis Ferdinand (1907–94), heir to the Imperial throne, never gave up his claim to the succession. It was through subversive circles around Goerdeler, Canaris, Oster and others that he propagated his aspirations to the throne. Goebbels never forgave him for using the traitor Otto John as an intermediary. The prince knew Otto John from their employment together at Lufthansa. John escaped from Germany to Britain where he joined Sefton Delmer and devoted himself to subversive propaganda and agitation against Germany. Goebbels often expressed to me the rancour he felt for Louis Ferdinand. After the war, Otto John returned to Germany to continue his career as a traitor. From the important

---

* The Hohenzollern dynasty reigned in Prussia from 1702 to 1918.

Office of Defence of the Constitution of the German Bundes-republik he worked secretly for the DDR until unmasked and sentenced to imprisonment.

For Goebbels, Auwi was an exception within the Imperial house. Even before he joined the Party on 1 April 1930, Goebbels described him on three occasions during 1930 (23 January, 2 February and 12 June) as 'a good man'. There is no doubt as to his sincerity in this. What linked the three of us emotionally, Adolf Hitler's Minister of Propaganda, the SA general of the Imperial house and myself, an SA private, is that each of us had intimate knowledge of the business end of a Weimar Republic police truncheon. I have described my own experience, but not those of Goebbels and the prince, who suffered his baptism in the same epoch, but in another region. Goebbels recalled it to me with humour and in detail although in his diary he limited it to a few words. On 21 March 1931 he noted: 'Yesterday ... Königsberg [capital of East Prussia] they forbade me to speak ... Auwi spoke ... at the railway station ... police ... truncheon ... Auwi also beaten ... threw me to the ground ... passed out ... furious. The truncheon used hard on someone, also on me.'

The three of us ran the gauntlet even if our personal levels were different. The brute force with which we were treated made us hard. Adolf Hitler also describes the phenomenon in his book. For that reason, millions of men from the most diverse social backgrounds, educational levels and ages stepped forward to serve. The body in Germany which united them all was called the SA.

CHAPTER 3

The Swastika on the Steel Helmet

It cannot be determined today when the SA came into existence. What is certain, however, is that it was a creation of the lost Great War. Nobody knows precisely who cut the umbilical cord and when. Beyond dispute is that the place of political birth was not Berlin, and much less its Lustgarten, but Munich, called until 1945 'The Capital of the Movement'.

This political creature was conceived on 9 November, five years before the march to the Feldherrnhalle in Munich and 71 years before the fall in 1989 of the Berlin Wall which the Marxist madness had erected to perpetuate indefinitely the division of Germany. On 9 November 1918, Social Democrat Philipp Scheidemann proclaimed the creation of a republic from a window of the Reichstag, the German parliament building in Berlin. A little before, Scheidemann had been appointed Secretary of State in the Imperial Cabinet of liberal Chancellor Prinz Max von Baden. This proclamation followed six days after the men at the Kiel naval base in the Baltic had mutinied against the Kaiser's government, while in the woods at Compiègne the Armistice negotiations commenced.

In Bavaria the previous day, a Leftist group had declared the breaking up of the Imperial Reich and the abandonment of the supposed Prussian protection. After violent local disorder, the Communists then proclaimed the 'Free State of Bavaria' on 8 November 1918. Curiously this title stuck and it has survived to the present day after being an integral part of the Third Reich and the Federal governments which succeeded it. Bavaria included the title formally in its provincial constitution of 1946.

The able orator and writer Kurt Eisner (1867–1919) established himself as the self-designated prime minister of the Bavarian government. He believed he should test the waters by calling democratic elections but was roundly defeated on 12 January 1919, his Social Democratic Independent Party obtaining only three of the 190 seats. The most numerous grouping continued to be the Bayerische Volkspartei (Bavarian People's Party) with sixty-six Catholic delegates. After 1945 the Christian Social Union (CSU) continued it. Eisner could never have governed democratically if it had been his intention to do, something for which there are grounds to doubt. Scarcely had the disastrous result become known than he struck up relations with the Workers' and Soldiers' Council, an organization dominated by revolutionary Marxists, which was in the process of planning to take power and proclaim a 'Republic of Bavarian Councils' on the Russian Soviet model.

He had no opportunity to conclude a pact with them, however, for while on his way to the Bavarian parliament with his resignation as prime minister in one pocket, and a proposal in favour of the Revolutionary Council of Workers and Soldiers in the other, he was gunned down in the street. His killer was a former Army officer, Anton Graf von Arco-Valley, identified as half-Jewish by the outstanding researcher into contemporaneous Bavarian history, Georg Franz-Willing, in his detailed three-volume work.* Arco received a relatively light sentence of five years' preventive detention, which he described in a book he wrote about his crime as soon as he got out.†

As soon as the Bavarian parliament heard of the Eisner assassination on 21 February 1919, utter chaos erupted. Scarcely

---

* Georg Franz-Willing, *Ursprung der Hitlerbewegung*, Preussisch-Oldendorf, 1974
† Anton Graf von Arco-Valley, *Aus fünf Jahren Festunghaft*, Regensburg, 1925.

had the leader of the Social Democrat majority, Eberhard Auer, finished a short speech expressing his proletarian indignation at the event than there occurred a scatter-brained shooting in which Auer was seriously wounded. The revolutionary ministers around him were left unharmed though shaken up, although two decorative figures of the advisory council were killed. The shooter escaped during the general panic and was later identified as a member of the Workers' Bolshevist Council named Linder, a butcher by trade. The leader responsible for 'military affairs' on the Council of the People's Delegates in Berlin (the new, but short-lived term for the War Minister) Gustav Noske (1868–1946) was convinced that there was a third party behind it. His suspicions could not be confirmed, but Noske, one of the most important personalities of the embryonic Weimar Republic, which was gradually consolidating, was put on his guard by the foregoing and other incidents which soon followed in the rebel Free State of Bavaria.

At this stage of the revolutionary events in Bavaria there appears for the first time a society surrounded by mystery and rumour: the Thule Gesellschaft, a Germanic Order, described by co-founder Rudolf von Sebottendorf on the day of its inauguration, 9 November 1918, as the beginning of 'spiritual purification after the happenings of yesterday, organized by inferior racial elements whose ultimate goal was to destroy Germanism'. The Thule Society, named after an island to the north (probably situated in the Shetlands archipelago), discovered and described in the fourth century before the Christan era by the navigator and geographer Pytheas, was the mythological cradle of National Socialism.* In those first years

---

* Pytheas (380–310 BC) was a Greek geographer and explorer who circumnavigated Britain in 330–320 BC. He was the first Graeco-Roman to describe the midnight sun, the aurora and polar ice, and the first to mention Germanic tribes. From his fragmentary chronicle 'On the Ocean' it is clear that fishermen already knew the Shetland and Orkney Isles, and Thule was near (*cont. on p. 34*)

of its existence whoever had name and rank came through the Thule Society. A central intellectual figure was the folkish poet Dietrich Eckart (1868–1923), whose name appears in the dedication at the end of Adolf Hitler's *Mein Kampf*.

Hitler himself was a marginal personality at the beginning, on a level equal to his later deputy in the National Socialist Party leadership, Rudolf Hess, or the man who drafted the Party manifesto, Gottfried Feder, the ideologist of the Movement Alfred Rosenberg, Reichswehr Hauptmann Ernst Röhm and the railway mechanic Anton Drexler who in 1919 founded the Deutsche Arbeiter Partei (DAP) which would later become the NSDAP of Hitler and his SA. On 9 November 1919 Sebottendorf had concluded the Thule Society's inaugural meeting with the significant and unmistakable words: 'And now we are going to speak of the German Reich, we are going to say that the Jew is our enemy, as from today we are going to act.' All knew to whom and to what he was referring.

After the murder of Eisner, his minister of culture, Hoffmann, formed a government in Bavaria consisting mainly of Social Democrats who, like their leader, were extreme-Left oriented and depended moreover on a Revolutionary Central Council. This was formed by the Jewish intellectuals Toller, Mühsam and Landauer who met regularly until the end of the Great War in the Café Stefani, nicknamed the 'café of the

(*cont. from p. 33*) neither. According to Pytheas it was an island six days' sail north of Britain and one days' sail south from the pack ice. It was an agricultural island whose inhabitants produced grain, honey, fruit and milk. No such balmy climate exists within the Arctic Circle and modern geographers therefore discount Pytheas, or put the island much closer to Britain. Dr Wilfried Dahm, biographer of Lanz von Liebenfels, co-founder of the Thule Society, stated in his book *Der Mann, der Hitler die Ideen gab*, (Munich, 1958), that the island is inhabited even in modern times by highly evolved beings. The real purpose of the Thule Society was to make a pact with these inhabitants to evolve humanity rapidly through the existing Germanic stock.

megalomaniacs' and located in the Schwabing district of Munich. The trio had joined up with the far-Left Imperial Navy rating, 23-year old Egelhofer, a mutineer at Kiel in November 1918, who was appointed some months later to command the 'Red Army' of Bavaria made up of deserters and common criminals. Inspired by tales from Hungary, where Béla Kun would operate a reign of terror at the behest of Lenin until 1920, the Schwabing Three proclaimed the grandiose Räterepublik (Bavarian Republic of Councils) on 7 April 1919. Hoffmann's legal government fled to Bamberg in the north of Bavaria and sought there the help of the Thule Society, which had been active and successful in setting up a number of paramilitary organizations. With the help of concerned Munich citizens Thule had established the Freikorps *Oberland* and equipped it well.

Toller and his associates made significant efforts to convert the Räterepublik into a madhouse, but fortunately only worked at it for a short period. 'The world must become a meadow filled with flowers,' they raved, 'in which each person can harvest his share.' An edict published by Landauer ruled: 'Everyone is now working in the manner which suits him best, everybody is equal to everybody else, legalistic thinking has ended.' Could anything be more absurd?

A few days afterwards, dedicated Communists took over the Spartacus group in Munich under the command of Max Lewien. A number of Russian Jews were involved such as Leviné-Niessen and Tobias Axelrod. Wilhelm Hoegner (1887–1980), for a time Social Democrat Prime Minister of Bavaria, referred in his book* to a political organization in his home province in which a number of Jews such as Leviné-Niessen, Wadler, Toller, Müsham and others played the predominant role. 'After the calamitous failure,' Hoegner wrote, 'the hatred of the Jews acquired dangerous dimensions.'

---

* Wilhelm Hoegner, *Die verratene Republik*, Munich, 1958

The Bolshevik murders of Thule Society members organized with the help of Egelhofer's 'Red Army' ensured the spread of that hate to the Reds after 26 April 1919. When a house was raided on a search warrant, anti-Communist and anti-Jewish literature was discovered. Of the approximately 200 members of the Thule Order only seven were caught, amongst them the society secretary, Heila Gräfin von Westarp. She and other Munich citizens were held hostage to protect the back of the Bolshevik government of Bavaria, in danger of collapse in the face of pressure by the population, beginning to arm, and the despatch of regular troops from Berlin.

Ten hostages, amongst them the seven Thule Society members, were murdered. Instead of being shot dead against a wall at the Luitpold College, then in use as a makeshift prison, they were beaten with rifle butts and then kicked to death. This occurred on 30 April 1919. These seven Thule members were the first to lose their lives for the emblem of the society, the swastika, well before the founding of the SA. Sebottendorf dedicated his book to them and their names will not be omitted here: Heila Gräfin von Westarp, Gustav Franz Maria Prinz von Thurn und Taxis, Franz Karl Freiherr von Teuchert, Friedrich Wilhelm Freiherr von Seydlitz, Anton Daumenland, Walter Deike, Walter Nauhaus.

Executions during wartime may be justified depending on the circumstances and were practised in effect by both sides, but in a civil war – above all one undertaken by those who have usurped power illegally, as did the Bolshevists in Munich – are a disgusting crime. The later summary trial and execution by shooting of Leviné-Niessen was justified and nobody wept for him. The co-author of the Luitpold College murders, Axelrod, was deported to Moscow, being a Russian citizen, where the trace disappears in the chaos reigning there at that time.

The fate of the Munich victims impressed me greatly. I was not yet seven but the death of my father at the front in Flanders had shocked me deeply and undoubtedly contributed to the making of my character. Heila von Westarp was not unknown to my family, although her ideological outlook was not shared or understood by all of them. There were several links by marriage between the von Westarps and the von Ovens. My great-great-grandfather Karl von Oven (1824–1907) had married Gräfin Emma von Westarp. In 1894 his daughter Godela married Adolf Graf von Westarp who lived in Munich until 1915. My mother had left Germany before the First World War after qualifying as a teacher, taking up a post as governess to a German family in La Paz. Here she met my father Kurt and married him, but she never had personal contact with Heila von Westarp. She knew a lot about her, though, for she confided much to the family. The terrible death of Heila affected me profoundly, following as it did within two years of the heroic death of her husband. We her children suffered for her.

The whole family was anxious for the future of its other members who, though lucky enough to have survived the war, now found themselves involved in one way or another in the revolutionary events in Germany. Apart from my father, his brother Oberstleutnant Udo von Oven (1866–1914) had fallen as commanding officer, Lifeguard Regiment No. 115 (First Grand Duke of Hesse), and also his son Leutnant Günter von Oven, Lifeguard Regiment No. 117 at the age of 19 on the Chemin des Dames near Laon.* All three perished on the Western Front.

Another of my uncles, my godfather Generalmajor Georg von Oven (1868–1938), was decorated with the Pour le Mérite for taking the Douaumont fortress at Verdun. Later he commanded a Freikorps formed for the purpose of putting down the Spartacist rising in Berlin. After having successfully completed this task, my uncle turned to religion and became a Protestant minister. His evangelical outpourings were singularly

* Alis von Schönermarck, *Helden-Gedenkmappe des deutschen Adels*, Stuttgart, 1921.

well-attended because he began and ended with a trumpet solo, the instrument being a family heirloom. The fact that I, Wilfred his godson, did not follow in his Christian footsteps wounded him deeply, and when, to make matters worse, I joined the SA in 1931, Uncle Georg considered it high time for a strong word, but to no avail. He died before the Third Reich was defeated, and as a recipient of the Pour le Mérite is buried in the Invalidenhof military cemetery in Berlin.

My godfather Georg was never a Nazi and had fewer public appearances of note than his cousin Ernst von Oven (1859–1945). When the Great War ended he was the highest-ranking officer in the German Army and as such the immediate direct subordinate to the Minister of Defence, Gustav Noske. From Noske he received the order to suppress the Marxist revolution in Bavaria and restore law and order in the Weimar Republic with whatever military units were available from the standing Army and the local Freikorps, civilian defence and similar bodies. Ernst von Oven carried out his orders without delay and thoroughly. He received no Pour le Mérite but he was not the man to thirst for decorations nor even expect any thanks. He did his duty even if his masters in Berlin were not totally in sympathy with it. The immediacy of his intervention against the Bolshevist terror in Munich, which had saved the tottering, fledgling Republic, was something which nobody in Berlin appeared to appreciate.

On the other side of the political divide my uncle's actions met the disapproval of the Right because ultimately he had saved the regime, and kept his comrades-in-arms from becoming embroiled in politics. It was for this reason that he remained on the sidelines during Kapp's coup d'état in March 1920.* In National Socialist propaganda and publicity, Ernst

---

* The Kapp Putsch was precipitated and ended in the following manner. In February 1920 the differences of opinion between Noske, Defence Minister in the Ebert government, and paramilitary reactionaries intensified. When the Inter-Allied Military Control

von Oven himself and his role in the recovery of Munich were minimized, if not suppressed. The man considered to be the liberator was Oberst (later General of the Army and SA) Franz Ritter von Epp, without doubt an honourable and respected officer who commanded various Freikorps, but who operated just as did all the other Freikorps and civilian defence units, under the orders of Reichswehr General Ernst von Oven. With his combined forces he had quickly put paid to the Red mess in Munich. On 30 April there occurred the massacre of the hostages at the Luitpold College; on 1 May Oven entered the city and soon held the Bavarian capital and had put the Red rabble, which had been responsible for so much spillage of blood and confusion, behind bars. That same day he advised the Social Democrat Minister Noske simply and succinctly: 'Munich is firmly in my hands.'

The family conversations we children overheard about the day to day occurrences moved us deeply. The concern could be seen reflected in our young faces. We no longer played at 'cops and robbers' or 'cowboys and Indians' as our fathers had done, but at 'Freikorps and Spartacus'. Of course, almost everybody wanted to be Freikorps, although there were a few who had not

Commission demanded the disbandment of naval brigades *Erhardt* and *Löwenfeld*, Noske ordered it for 10 March. At the first anniversary reunion of Brigade *Erhardt* on 1 March the members declared they would rather topple the government than disband. On 10 March when General Lüttwitz, commander of the naval brigades, refused to disband them he was relieved of command and arrest warrants were issued for the conspirators. These were tipped off beforehand by the police and went into hiding. On 13 March Brigade *Erhardt* occupied the government district in Berlin and Wolfgang Kapp declared himself prime minister. The Putsch collapsed on 17 March due to the uncompromising attitude of the President, government and the Reichswehr generals, including Oven; the refusal of naval ratings to obey Admiral von Trotha and their officers and support the coup; and major strikes in the larger cities. Michael Müller, *Canaris*, pp. 106–9.

yet got the point. Our small neighbour Frederika whined: 'I want to be a Spartacist.' We let her, but she knew nothing of the Marxist atrocities, particularly those committed in Munich. In our house the situation was different. The fate of Heila von Westarp and the other hostages murdered at the Luitpold College, and the service of my two uncles against the Spartacist revolutionaries, were subjects of everyday discussion in the bosom of our family. It bound us together for all our lives.

In Germany itself, the three following generations were re-modelled by indoctrination so deeply and unscrupulously that nowadays few know of the trials and tribulations which the German people went through immediately after the First World War. For that reason I place my childhood memories and impressions at the beginning of this book and will come back to them again in a subsequent chapter. Whether one admires or condemns it, the SA as an organization for political struggle was, with its four million members, a singular entity, unique in Germany and perhaps in world history. I marched in its ranks. I never denied it, nor was ashamed to confess it, and not simply because at Nuremberg postwar, the victors' tribunals declared the SA to be 'not a criminal organization'.

We all wore the swastika, but only those who in 1923 were incorporated by Röhm into the escort unit for the march to the Feldherrnhalle (organized into a regiment by Göring in 1934 and renamed Regiment *Feldherrnhalle*) were allowed to wear the swastika on the steel helmet. The 'swastika on the steel helmet' had been the holy emblem and mark of Naval Brigade *Erhardt*, a unit formed by that Imperial Navy officer at the end of the Great War, and excellently led. The tune for the lyrics of 'Swastika on the Steel Helmet' was a simple but catchy melody. The SA absorbed it as its own (plagiarism!) composed its own lyrics for the final part, substituting 'Hitler's SA' for 'Brigade Erhardt'. We sang it heartily if not too tunefully. But which of us knew anything about Kapitän zur See Erhardt?

The Bavarian historian Georg Franz-Willing described 'Brigade *Erhardt*' as 'the mother organization of the SA'* and for that reason Kapitän Erhardt is justly considered to be the father. Erhardt was never a National Socialist. He was an exceptional officer, a nationalist and a loyal subject of the Kaiser. The swastika and the colours black-white-red, both elements adopted initially by the SA and then the Reich, were not his invention. The swastika dates back in German history to the Bronze Age and in Asia (from where the word 'swastika' originated from the Sanskrit), to three millenia before the Christian era. The colours were devised by Bismarck to unite the black and white of Prussia with the red of the Hanseatic League. Erhardt was therefore not supplying anything new to the assault troop of the embryonic NSDAP, but something traditional and conservative. He had been 33 when first seeing action as an officer of the Imperial Navy while the first SA men seven years later were aged from 17 to 23. The exclusively nationalist–conservative feelings which motivated Erhardt were not to be expected of the young SA men who were above all revolutionaries in the social sphere. Erhardt never became an ideological teacher but was the organizer and military mentor of the expanding SA. Beyond supplying good advice, he put at its disposition his most suitable officers. The first leader of a regular SA troop in Munich, as from August 1921, was Kapitänleutnant Hans Ulrich Klintzsch, an officer with Brigade *Erhardt*, after the leader of the small NSDAP, Adolf Hitler, had created on 3 August that year a troop to protect the political rallies camouflaged as a sporting association and known as Turn und Sport Abteilung.

Klintzsch had resigned his commission in June 1921 to study in Munich. Subsequently he joined the NSDAP. His name appeared for the first time in a proclamation published in edition No. 24 of the *Völkischer Beobachter* entitled 'To Our

* Franz-Willing, *Ursprung der Hitlerbewegung.*

German Youth'. It removed from the new formation all appearance of being inoffensive, calling it 'the battering ram' of the Movement, it being an easy transition from there to its later and final name, Sturmabteilung or SA. Its mission was to protect the indoctrination process by Nazi propagandists which Hitler had arranged for at its creation.

Klintzsch had not yet cast aside military customs for his new civilian surroundings. In his article he stated that the Turn und Sport Abteilung he led would be the 'military bastion' of a free people. This was not of course exactly what Adolf Hitler was hoping for from the SA. There were many 'military bastions' in Germany, mainly in Bavaria: he wanted 'political soldiers' like himself, who had spent four years in the trenches at the front and then turned his hand to political instruction for the young Reichswehr, in which he continued to serve and receive pay. Therefore the Turn und Sport Abteilung had to be something else. Hitler wanted to bind strong, healthy men educated in his doctrine into a force to end the Marxist terror. More important for him than military instruction and target shooting was sports training, boxing and jiu-jitsu, the forerunner to modern karate. He describes this in *Mein Kampf*.

Many of his early followers were comrades from the front; others had been soldiers, but from other units. Amongst the first SA chiefs, besides Klintzsch, were Kapitän zur See Alfred Hoffmann, Oberleutnant Wilhelm Brückner, Leutnant Rudolf Hess (who founded and led the 'Company of Militant Students'), Leutnant Wegelin, Leutnant Baldenius, Major Streck and finally Hauptmann Hermann Göring who, at the beginning of 1923, became leader of the SA but was seriously wounded during the march to the Feldherrnhalle. In the second volume of his book, Hitler relates that there were many former comrades from the trenches amongst his early followers. Soon they would know another kind of struggle, man-to-man, but with fists rather than bayonets.

In October 1919, the Marxists attempted to break up a political meeting in the Eberlbräukeller. 'Like a swarm of wasps the SA hurled itself on the demonstrators', he wrote, 'who then fell down the stairs with bumps on their heads.'* Something similar but more serious was repeated during the demonstration of 24 February 1920 at the popular Hofbräuhaus tavern when the Red rabble, which had tried a few months previously to test its strength against the political movement, made a fresh and unsuccessful attempt. The small but vigorous and well-trained SA team, recruited by Emil Maurice from amongst people sympathetic to his ideology and to whom he had given training in unarmed combat, were victorious, demonstrating to the adversary that they were no easy meat. These young men who defended the Party meetings had learnt from their leader that 'terror must be met with terror' and that 'in this world only the brave and the resolute win the laurels', as Hitler would write much later in *Mein Kampf* during his spell at Landsberg Prison.

Maurice demonstrated the art of putting words into practice even though, as a watchmaker, his hands were not made for fisticuffs. In the trenches he had exchanged the watchmaker's pincers and eye-glass for the machine-gun and stick grenade. Born in 1897, he had already surpassed the upper age limit of the association without anybody noticing it. He had set the limit himself. A short while before becoming a self-defence instructor he had a brief stay at the *Völkischer Beobachter*. His model was Hitler's personal bodyguard, Ulrich Graf, often called 'the first SA man', although much later he joined the other organization to fit the circumstances, the SS.

Another man who can be considered one of the first SA men is Julius Schaub, who succeeded Graf as Hitler's keeper after Graf was wounded on the march to the Feldherrnhalle. Later Schaub became Hitler's personal adjutant in whose immediate

* Adolf Hitler, *Mein Kampf*, Munich, 1933, p. 551.

proximity he remained until 23 April 1945. I had the chance to know him when I accompanied my principal, Dr Goebbels, at meetings he had with Hitler at his *Wolfsschanze* headquarters in East Prussia. There I would run into Schaub every time Hitler and Goebbels conferred. While our respective heads met, Schaub and I had nothing else to do but dedicate ourselves to the culinary delights in the tea pavilion. Schaub was not one to disdain strong drink. His only mission in life was to be at Hitler's beck and call. He was the sole keyholder for the strongboxes in Hitler's various offices. From the safe in the Reich Chancellery – Hitler's last refuge – he removed the Führer's personal papers which had been ordered burnt, and a medium calibre Walther pistol.

The last time I met Schaub before 22 April 1945 I told him that Dr Goebbels had given me the private papers from his desk for burning in Schaub's presence in the hearth at his office on Berlin's Hermann Göring-Strasse. Also photos of his great love, the Czech actress Lida Baarova. Shortly after Goebbels had taken his leave of me on 22 April 1945 to move with his family into the Chancellery bunkers where he, his wife and their six young children met their tragic end, Schaub destroyed the personal papers of Adolf Hitler by fire.

I thought a lot of Schaub, who had been aged 33 when I joined the SA at age 19. He was always concerned for our physical well-being when we had to report to Führer HQ. He was rather like the butler to the ministerial secretaries and attachés and maintained a relaxed relationship in the ante-chambers of the Reich. He was the longest-serving man in his post – over a quarter century from 1919 to 1945 – but never part of Hitler's intimate circle. He never addressed Hitler by the intimate pronoun '*Du*'. Only Emil Maurice and Röhm ever did so. When Hitler was released from prison in December 1924 and had begun to play a certain political role after the ban on the Party was lifted, he employed his friend and comrade

Maurice as his chauffeur and, after 1933, appointed him a Councillor in Munich.

Hitler and Maurice, Erhardt and Klintzsch, Hess and Röhm, all these men and many others from the early days had been soldiers and acted as such when, after the war ended, they began organizing the National Socialist Movement and the SA from Bavaria. Without the SA, the NSDAP would never have gained power. Many of them, Hitler and Röhm included, served in the Reichswehr created after 1918 by the new Weimar Republic and received their pay from that source. This fact has led many naive young historians – the products of a perverse re-education policy – to reason that this was the converse of Clausewitz's dictum 'War is simply the continuation of state policy by other means'. Thus for example, Peter Longerich wrote in his previously mentioned book *Die braunen Bataillonen*: 'The militarization of politics, that is to say, the continuation of organized violence learnt and practised during the war, carried over into internal political differences – those were the tangible conditions which impregnated the SA in its initial phase.'

The facts are as simple and straightforward as that nowadays for many re-educated fellow citizens. But this is a common fundamental error committed by the historian who is distant from events and has fallen prey to 'democratic' propaganda. In the following pages I shall demonstrate that fact.

It is true that we wore the 'swastika on the steel helmet' of the legendary Brigade *Erhardt*, but the millennias-old symbol of Germanic man was for us youths of the SA more important and formative than the helmet. The war forced us to wear the steel helmet, but on our heads for protection, and not in our hearts, as the democratic re-educators would have us believe today.

CHAPTER 4

Iron Cross – Iron Fist – Iron Front

Adolf Hitler had discovered his talent for oratory before forming the bodyguard for his protection during speech-making, and so enable the eloquent delivery of his message. Until the last moment of the Great War, the only thing which the modest Austrian private had had the opportunity to say was '*Jawohl*' when he received the orders of his superiors. Six months later at the Army's No. 4 Command, Bavaria, courses were begun for men capable of influencing the armed forces for the purpose of re-establishing national discipline. (During the Second World War, Army propaganda companies were responsible for this task.)

In Munich the job of education was run by Department Ib/P commanded by retired General Staff Hauptmann Karl Mayr. Sifting through the candidates for the courses, his attention was drawn to a private who had been awarded the Iron Cross First and Second Class. These decorations on the simple field-grey jacket of a common soldier promised that the wearer was a brave man who loved the Fatherland. Hitler's accent, as a native of the Austro-Bavarian border, was familiar to the ears of South Germans.

He had only had a secondary school education, although this could be made up for in other ways. Gefreiter Hitler, who was still drawing Army pay plus bed and food, passed the course to the entire satisfaction of his superiors. In August 1919 he was sent to an indoctrination unit at Lechfeld military camp near Augsburg, where Marxist infiltration was very

marked. He was to administer the antidote. His unit
commander, Oberleutnant Bendt, confirmed that the mentally
agile private had done his work well. The historian and former
SA General Heinrich Bennecke confirmed in his book that
'Hitler explained to the men the various modules in a fervid
and comprehensible manner.'*

The highly praised orator-in-the-making confessed in *Mein
Kampf*: 'No duty could have made me happier than this one.'
He performed it 'with heart and soul', and that was the secret
of his success. He realized that he 'could speak'. Again he relates
in his book: 'Hundreds, maybe thousands of comrades found
the way back to our people and Fatherland through my
speeches.' Many of them, he continued, formed 'the original
membership of the new Movement'.

One of the mentors who helped Hitler become an ideological
instructor was the historian and journalist Karl Alexander von
Müller (b. 1882), a well-known personality at the turn of the
century and from 1914 a publisher of the monthly *Süddeutsche
Monatshefte*. He authored a variety of historical works and his
memoirs *Mars und Venus* appeared in 1957. It was Müller who
suggested to Hauptmann Mayr that he should have a look at
Hitler. Within No. 4 Command of the Reichswehr at Munich,
Mayr was engaged in something akin to propaganda work. The
captain was so pleased with the 'propagandist apprentice' that
he addressed a letter to the private soldier 'Very esteemed Herr
Hitler'. One such letter bears the date 10 September 1919 and
appears in Ernst Röhm's book *A Traitor's Story*,[†] also
mentioned by Bennecke.

It was Mayr who introduced Hitler to Röhm in 1920. This
occurred during a secret meeting of nationalist officers to which
Hitler had been invited. This secret Rightist circle was called
the Eiserne Faust (Iron Fist). Its political influence was meagre
but brought Hitler and Röhm together. They became close

* Heinrich Bennecke, *Hitler und die SA*, Munich, 1962.
† Ernst Röhm, *Geschichte eines Hochverräters*, Munich, 1934.

friends and used the familiar pronoun *Du* when addressing each other. A little later, in mid-1920, Mayr resigned from the Army and disappeared from the National Socialist scene in the Bavarian capital. It is a curious fact that it was he who would create the impetus for the Movement by promoting people such as Hitler and other important members of the new party. The rumour that Mayr was a spy or agent of the Socialist regime in Berlin who had been infiltrated into the Reichswehr was apparently confirmed in 1924 when Socialists Hörsing and Höltermann founded Reichsbanner Schwarz-Rot-Gold (Black-Red-Gold Reich Banner) just when it was forseen that the ban on the NSDAP, imposed after the failed coup of 9 November 1923 was about to be lifted. The chief of the general staff of Reichsbanner, which had more than three million Marxist acolytes when Hitler took power in 1933, was none other than the ex-admirer of the new Reich Chancellor, retired Hauptmann Karl Mayr.

To be honest, we SA men of the early 1930s did not take very seriously these millions of the Marxist revolutionary army. Much more dangerous than Mayr's 'club for a banana republic', as we labelled it ironically, was 'Teddy' Thälmann's (1886–1944) 'Fighting League of the Red Front.'

The political conglomeration created at the beginning of the 1930s for the 'Imperial Standard' under the pompous name Eiserne Front (Iron Front), whose aim was to stop the National Socialist advance, was really more cardboard than iron and we enjoyed facing up to it. Nowadays opportunist politicians avoid speaking of Mayr and his evolution from 'Iron Cross' through 'Iron Fist' to 'Iron Front'. Peter Longerich of the Institute of Contemporary History never mentions him when actually one cannot overstress the enormous help Mayr lent Hitler in the early stages of his political career. Equally, Longerich prefers to remain silent on the important support which the conservative groups gave National Socialism and its fighting arm, the SA.

When we marched through the working-class districts of Berlin we used to shout: 'Germany awake!' At times standing in rented lorries, our flag fluttering in the wind, our company commander Riewe, a giant of six foot six would roar in his enormous voice: '*Deutschland!*' and we would chorus '*Erwache!*' And this had the desired effect, because Germany awoke.

That slogan was not invented by us, having already been in current use for forty years. Dr Alfred Hugenberg (1865–1951) had made it popular in 1892 as a co-founder of the Pan-German Association. The DAP (German Workers' Party) founded by the railway mechanic Anton Drexler, taken to the summit much later by Hitler, had been part of the Pan-German Association. Its other prominent members were Dietrich Eckart, Alfred Rosenberg and Julius Streicher. As contemporary history likes to forget both Hauptmann Mayr and the millionaire Hugenberg, I shall describe briefly the latter's brilliant career up to 1933, and his political end.

Alfred Hugenberg had begun his successful professional life in the Imperial Reich where he was a consultant for the Prussian Ministry of the Economy. Before and during the Great War he was chairman of the board of the Krupp empire at Essen, and it was during this epoch that he began organizing his own firms, of which the Scherl editorial house and the cinematic producer UFA were acquiring a form of monopoly on information. Shortly after the revolution of 1918, he was elected as a Reichstag deputy for the Deutsch-Nationale Volkspartei, and in 1928 was leader of the same. In that role he offered to form a common front, Harzburg, with Hitler, the aim being to seize power jointly. This merger was the reason why I quit the SA and Nazi Party.

Just as Hitler had organized the SA 'battering ram' for his political party, the Social Democrats (SPD) prepared their own paramilitaries – with the active participation of Hauptmann Karl Mayr – under the colours of the Reichsbanner.

Hugenberg's trusted formations consisted of members of the Stahlhelmbund der Front Soldaten founded at Magdeburg on 13 November 1918 by Franz Seldte (1882–1947), and for the millions of adherents who made up Stahlhelm, Seldte, its first President, was the model of military virtue. He had lost an arm in the war and wore the Iron Cross, First and Second Class.

Basically Stahlhelm had been created as a simple traditionalist organization but was rapidly increasing its sphere of action to the point that it was able to intervene in the armed defence of the German population of Silesia against Polish incursions, in the Ruhr against a French invasion and in Central Germany against the Communist disorder. Without any doubt Stahlhelm acted in an exemplary manner and reinforced the national feelings of the people. The SA maintained good, comradely relations with the war veterans because originally Stahlhelm had been composed exclusively of old soldiers. They felt, evidently, the pride in their uniforms that seemed like those worn at the front.

From 1924 its ranks began to fill with youths who had never been soldiers, and thus it avoided delapidating into a club for 'old fossils'. Their military drill seemed to us ridiculous, particularly when they taught 'Present arms!' with walking sticks in place of rifles, but all the same they were feared by their adversaries when putting across their point of view. At first sight it all looked like a childish game of paper helmets and wooden swords. This was the Stahlhelm which Hugenberg paraded in 1931 for the political marriage with Nazism. Hitler gave him a ministry after taking power in 1933 in recognition of his sacrifice. Hugenberg resigned office on 28 June 1933 but remained a Reichstag deputy to the last day of the war. He played no further political role before his death on 12 March 1951.

The Stahlhelm president, Franz Seldte was a member of Hitler's Cabinet along with Hugenberg, and ran the Ministry of Labour until the end of the war, although some sections were the responsibility of others. Fritz Sauckel ran the labour force while Robert Ley coordinated the only permitted trade union, the Arbeitsfront. The Allied victors, punctilious in everything, never forgave Seldte: his crime had been to accept the rank of SA general and incorporate Stahlhelm into the SA. He died in Allied internment on 1 April 1947.

The most capable Stahlhelm man was undoubtedly Max Jüttner. As a professional soldier he had served in the Imperial Army from 1906 to 1920, and after, for a short time, with the Weimar Republic. Once Germany had been demilitarized, Jüttner worked as a coal miner in his local region, central Germany. This was a Red environment, and Jüttner was probably unique amongst his fellow unionists in being a member of Hugenberg's Deutsch-Nationale Volkspartei and also Stahlhelm. He progressed professionally and eventually became a company agent. Politically he distanced himself from Hugenberg but not Stahlhelm, of which he was regional president. As such he is mentioned by the future Gauleiter Rudolf Jordan in his description of the seizure of power in the province of Halle-Merseburg.[*]

While the SA brown battalions marched on the evening of 30 January 1933 in torchlight procession through the Brandenburg Gate towards the Old Chancellery building, in the traditional Hallmarkt of the provincial capital Halle the masses assembled to hear the inspired oratory on national awakening delivered by local Stahlhelm leader Max Jüttner. When he expressed his satisfaction that Germany now had, in Adolf Hitler, a political soldier at the head of government, the public burst into a frenzy of enthusiasm. These were not merely words spoken to the wind. This Jüttner would demonstrate to the Nuremberg tribunals between 13 and 16 August 1946, as will be explained in the next chapter.

[*] Rudolf Jordan, *Erlebt und erlitten*, Leoni, 1971

CHAPTER 5

Patriots or Criminals?

As Stahlhelm chief for the Central Germany region, Jüttner was summoned before the Nuremberg military tribunal not as a defendant but to give testimony. The tribunal was presided over by British judge Sir Geoffrey Lawrence. Following delivery of his personal details, the judge set out the description of Jüttner's activities thus. In November 1933, that is to say after Hitler had taken charge of the government by legal means, the witness began to collaborate with the SA national leadership whose head was Ernst Röhm. In mid-1934 Jüttner joined the Nazi Party and was appointed nominal head of the central office, Hauptamt Führung der SA, a post he held to the end of the war. He was therefore the witness most competent in the matter of the integration of Stahlhelm into the SA.

His declarations coincided exactly with those of the previous Stahlhelm leader, its founder Franz Seldte. The organization had about a million members at the time, or perhaps rather more, according to the witness. More than half, some 550,000, were in favour of the merger with the SA, perhaps not all voluntarily, but they were not forced to agree. In any case, a minority of Stahlhelm members did not want to cast aside the field-grey Army-type uniform for the brown of the SA.

I was never 'invited', much less forced, to return to the ranks of the SA after resigning in 1932, although there was a tentative encouragement to do so: Hitler had decided not to accept any further requests for Party membership except from SA members. The avalanche of applications had overwhelmed the physical capacity of the Party employees. The numerical increase which the SA experienced in the 1933–4 period was greater than that known by any political movement previously: from 300,000 to 3,500,000 members! By the outbreak of war in 1939, another million had joined. Jüttner could not give the precise figure because the records had been destroyed during Allied air raids, but of one thing he could be sure and could swear to the military tribunal 'with a totally clear conscience and under oath' – all these millions of men, and their millions of family members, never had, not even remotely, any criminal character.

The prosecuting attorney-judges (combined in the single role!) were forced to accept that what Jüttner claimed was true. Worse than the accusations of the enemy for Jüttner were the slanders of the German traitor Hans Bernd Gisevius, who called the SA a criminal organization and 'gangsters'. To prove the lie which, elsewhere, continues a life of its own in the modern official histories, Jüttner gave the percentage of SA criminals held by the Allies in internment as 0.65 per cent, a figure which was never challenged. This meant that only one in every 150 members had been convicted of any offence worse than a misdemeanour. This was significantly lower than the criminality of the population at large which was 1.67 per cent according to the official statistics.

Gisevius died in 1974 without ever having succeeded in refuting Jüttner's claim made before the IMT at Nuremberg. In contrast to the former Stahlhelm–SA leader, Gisevius's deplorable role as traitor and Allied spy during the Second World War came to light. At the end of the Great War he was 14, the son of a solid middle-class lawyer and deputy leader of Hugenberg's patriotic organization for juveniles. When Hitler seized power, Gisevius had already completed his law studies, and applied to join the Nazi Party before the closing date. He was one of those opportunists we used to refer to contemptuously as 'The Fallen in March' (an expression coined after the democratic revolution of March 1848) or also 'The March violets' (which flower for a few days and then rapidly wither). Immediately afterwards, he applied successfully for a post with the government of Prussia and was transferred to the political branch of the Berlin police, with which we of the SA had had many bad experiences during the epoch in question, and worked intensively with the Gestapo at organizing its structure. He managed to unseat his immediate superior Rudolf Diels, but was not appointed to replace him.

As a *Regierungsrat* (government adviser) he had to content himself during the Second World War with a position in the military Abwehr run by the traitor-admiral Canaris, the man responsible for proposing that the Jews wear the 'Star of David' patch on their clothing. Once unfrocked Canaris was executed for high treason together with others on 9 April 1945. Gisevius was not amongst them, being safe and sound in the Swiss Alps. The 'Resistance' had packed him off there disguised as a vice-consul, where he was to contact Allen Dulles, head of the American OSS intelligence organization in Berne. He did his job well, but when things seemed to be progressing nicely towards the coup d'état to be attempted on 20 July 1944, he returned quickly to Berlin so as 'not to miss the bus', just as he had done on 30 January 1933. Gisevius dodged the hangman and while his country was being reduced to rubble by dozens of enemy nations, whom he helped all he could, he was enjoying Swiss cheese and chocolate in the country of their manufacture.

The Nuremberg trials were a mockery of a judicial system. While Gisevius's compatriots and the organizations of which they formed part – and which he had at one time hastened to join – were receiving justice from the victors' prosecuting attorney-judges, Gisevius was there as a political observer and prosecution witness. With the material he collected, in 1946 he turned out a book *Bis zum bitteren Ende* which became a best-seller in the re-educationalist end of the market.

For us old comrades of the former SA general, the deportment of Max Jüttner, as much towards the traitor Gisevius as the whole proceedings at Nuremberg, was a cause for immense joy and pride. He not only refuted the lies of our enemies and their docile German helpers, but replied correctly and firmly to all questions put to him. Thus he explained the phenomenal growth of the SA after 1933 as already described. Once the war broke out in 1939, the numbers dropped by 1.5 million. Although the SA was an enormous organization with a membership of over 4.5 million men, before September 1939 its political influence was minimal, if not totally absent, especially after the Röhm affair of 30 June 1934. This was evident for the professional career of a number of its leaders. Röhm himself, whom Jüttner described at Nuremberg as a man of strong personality, was appointed a minister shortly after the seizure of power in 1933, but had no portfolio. His successor, Viktor Lütze, was made a *Reichsleiter*, but also without portfolio, and exercised no influence on government business. Finally Schepmann, the last SA head, was neither minister nor *Reichsleiter*.

As a witness, Jüttner had, as head of the Hauptamt Führung der SA (SA Leadership Main Office), a well-founded knowledge of every SA commander. He did not deny that amongst this host were a number of total incompetents who had had to be separated out, but they were 'in an absolute minority', as he expressed during cross examination on 13 August 1946. Of the SA career chiefs, whose private, professional, political lives and ethics he had been obliged to examine, he had not uncovered a single 'failure'. All had qualified for and practised a civilian profession before entering the SA. In comparison to similar posts in public or private administration, their remuneration was modest. Nobody got rich in the SA by virtue of his post. In his summary, Jüttner stated: 'The main body of the SA directorship was decent and clean and in their way of interpreting affairs just and responsible, without a stain.'

In this respect Jüttner's observation was important where he pointed out that until 1933 there were no salaried posts at all within the SA, a statement clearly at odds with the views of the guild of 'modern historians' who attribute the enormous growth in the SA to the material benefits received by associates! The contrary is true. For my own part, I can swear that during my period of SA militancy I never received a single pfennig, not even to reimburse expenses, all of which had to be funded out of my own pocket. At times, and in certain circumstances, the women of the NS-Frauenschaft made sandwiches for us. I shall never forget the fat sausage-roll one of these female Samaritans gave me at Berlin-Lichtenrade when, during a Party rally on the speakers' dais with other comrades, I fainted with hunger.

To return to the Nuremberg tribunals and upright witness Max Jüttner. Under cross-examination he stated that before 1933 only a few of the leaders found a subsidy in the regulations to alleviate some of their expenses, no more than 300 RM monthly, and only then providing the regional cashiers had loose petty cash. After 1933 a proper salary scale was introduced from the rank of SA-Obersturmbannführer upwards, the maximum remuneration being 1,200 RM monthly. It was not a great deal, and much less than has been alleged. Only 2 per cent of SA leaders were salaried; the others gave their services *ad honorem*. Their honour was to defend the Fatherland. More than half the senior ranks in the SA in 1939 from Standartenführer upwards fell in action. Jüttner concluded this part of his testimony with the following words: 'I feel great pride in having belonged to that great institution.' I confess, as an ex-SA man who could not participate in the tribunal proceedings either as an observer and less so as a witness, since I was obliged to live anonymously and under a false name,

I should probably have broken out in frenetic applause at hearing these words ...

At a certain point, Max Jüttner's attorney, Böhm, asked the president of the tribunal if his client could make a declaration. The judge enquired: 'In relation to what matter does your client wish to make this declaration?' Jüttner replied swiftly, 'As to whether the SA committed war crimes or crimes against humanity.' The defending advocate, intervening briefly, stressed the importance of the matter and the judge agreed, providing that the witness was brief. Former SA general Max Jüttner then made the following sworn statement, which is taken directly from the transcripts:

> We, the men of the SA, did nothing evil. We neither wanted the war nor did we plan it. We did that which all the world considers to be an ethical and moral obligation: defend the Homeland and preserve the peace. We committed no crimes of any kind against humanity and it is for that reason that we ask no forgiveness, even less mercy. All we ask for is justice. Our consciences are clear, we acted as patriots. But if it is the intention to brand patriots as criminals, then we were criminals.

The witness then stepped down. The verdict pronounced on the SA on 30 September 1946 reads:

> One cannot say that its members participated in criminal acts, nor even that they knew of them. Therefore this tribunal considers it inappropriate to declare the SA a criminal organization within the meaning of Article 9 of the Statute.

The Nuremberg verdict spared millions of men and their families from persecution and maltreatment. It gave me no peace or feeling of relief, however. I had served to the end the last Chancellor of the Third Reich, Dr Joseph Goebbels, whom we of the SA had once chaired on our shoulders. It remains for me a heavy burden to this day, and resulted in the German Embassy in Buenos Aires branding me a Nazi and *persona non grata*. I accept it with indifference and in certain knowledge that the coming century will confirm the verdict passed on Hitler's brown battalions at Nuremberg.

CHAPTER 6

Who Defends the Reich?

The destiny of the SA was decided by the answer to this question in a manner which today can be considered tragic. When Adolf Hitler entered the Harzburg Front pact with Hugenberg and the Stahlhelm, he committed himself to support the Reichswehr as the only legitimate armed force of the nation should he take power. This was an agreement sworn to under oath and before the Supreme Court at Leipzig. Röhm, Supreme SA-Führer, had another opinion. He wanted the SA to be a popular National Socialist army in the future Third Reich. As an ex-officer of the Imperial Reich active after 9 November 1918, he wore the cockade and epaulettes on his uniform with pride and, continuing in the rank of captain in the army of the Weimar Republic, he strove to organize that political body according to strict military principles.

Hitler knew Röhm's intentions and, although he did not approve of them, he did not reject them expressly, even less forbid them. It was not new military formations which he needed. There existed more than enough of these in the first postwar years, principally in Bavaria. He wanted a formation, not necessarily armed, but with quality military training and discipline, which would provide order and protection for his political activities. For the purpose of avoiding a clash, and to implement his idea smoothly, Hitler did not openly oppose Röhm's ambitions. In the enemy camp the Social Democrats acted likewise in not opposing the activities of Hauptmann Mayr and his 'club for a banana republic'.

The exclusive right to bear arms had not been the primary objective in 1919 when National Socialism came into being. Arms were accessible in adequate quantities. The German Army, which had withdrawn from the field undefeated, had returned home with all its equipment. The enemy had not confiscated much. The 100,000 men which the Dictate of Versailles had permitted the vanquished as a standing army was not short of armaments even if they were not the most modern. The German authorities handling disarmament had managed to salt away the greatest possible quantity: after all, one never knew when they might be needed again.

Röhm had earned the nickname 'king of the Bavarian machine gun'. He knew and administered the secret local Reichswehr arsenals and handled weapons distribution. This fact, and his undoubted talent for organization, made him Hitler's most important collaborator before the NSDAP was banned in November 1923. Despite their divergent opinions on the role of the SA, their personal relationship did not suffer. Röhm and the other SA commanders saw the organization primarily as a military instrument. For Hitler, the SA was a tool for popular agitation, for massive demonstrations, to defend rallies, hand out leaflets, and so on.

On 4 November 1921 the SA, still known as a sporting association, received its baptism of brawling in the saloons of the Hofbräuhaus. Hitler described the event in detail in his second book. He had found out that the opposition was to riot at the meeting because the Red leaders, syndicalists from manufacturing establishments, were seeing their political ambitions melt as the new movement heated up. For this reason they formed a militant group composed principally of hard men from the locomotive factory and other large Munich companies.

The hall filled early, and the police shut the doors before the appointed time. Not all the protection Hitler had requested arrived in time: forty-five or forty-six men got in, he believed, according to his book. Maurice and Hess led them, a sorry group compared with hundreds of Communists already inside lusting to hand out 'a proletarian lesson' to the brownshirts. The 'proletarian lesson' began late. Hitler had been speaking for ninety minutes, and while doing so had noticed the opposition ordering endless glass mugs of beer. As well as lending Dutch courage by their contents, these mugs were splendid artillery. The signal was given, the glasses began to fly, chairs were smashed for parts to reinforce the proletarian argument and Hitler looked on as this 'stupid spectacle' unfolded. There was some shooting and people fell wounded but none died. The battle ended when the last Marxist fled. Just as if this brawl had been nothing more than a musical intermezzo, the chairman of the meeting, Hermann Esser,* announced that the function would resume, and with great pomp invited the 'lecturer', as Hitler was called at the time, to proceed with his discourse.

The first battle in a closed hall had been concluded successfully. In this way the 'sporting association' was transformed into the SA (Sturmabteilung – Assault Brigade), a name which stuck. The SA would have many such 'battles within four walls' across the Reich until 1933, and particularly in Berlin. In the capital, the equivalent of the Hofbräuhaus (an enormous tavern with numerous saloons which remains in business today and enjoys world fame) was the Bock brewery on Fidicin-Strasse.

The first battle in a public thoroughfare by which the SA won its 'right to the street', until then the exclusive prerogative of the Reds, occurred the following year, also in Munich. In April 1922, Germany and the Soviet Union signed the Rapallo Accord (Rapallo is a town in Liguria near Genoa). It was mutually agreed not to demand reparations in wars fought against each other. Chancellor Wirth and Foreign Minister

* Hermann Esser (1900–81), at the end of his career a National Socialist Secretary of State in the Propaganda Ministry.

Walter Rathenau signed for Germany. Modern historical research has described this accord as the first step by the defeated Germany, bound hand and foot, towards a kind of political independence. The man responsible for negotiating this deal, Rathenau, was shot dead less than two months later when proceeding to his office. The assassins were members of the Consul group, a branch of Brigade *Erhardt*.

The Weimar Republic* reacted to this assassination with all the rigour allowed it by the notorious 'Law to Protect the Republic' which over the next ten years gave it the legal wherewithal to outlaw arbitrarily virtually everything attempted by the nationalist opposition. The state of Bavaria refused to implement the Law after various patriotic groups organized a massive demonstration in the main square in Munich on 16 August 1922. The young Munich SA participated with its first 600 centurions. During the march to the square they unfurled for the first time their swastika flags. As yet they had not been issued uniforms and wore civilian 'vagabond' attire. Skirmishes ensued with Marxists. Until that moment the Reds had never given up their claim to exclusive rights over the streets, but now with heads bloodied, they were forced to give ground, as Hitler described in *Mein Kampf*.

The demonstration was reportedly attended by 60,000 persons and went off without any major trouble, being hailed as a resounding success. The positive outcome of this demonstration encouraged Hitler to plan another two months later which was more provocative than the first. At Coburg on the border with Thuringia, which had just been annexed to Bavaria by plebiscite, various nationalist groups had decided to hold a rally, on 'German Day', 14–15 October 1922. The fledgling NSDAP had been invited to participate, led by its

---

* The Weimar Republic (1919–33) in Germany was so called because the inaugural parliamentary assembly of post-Imperial Germany had to be held at the beginning of 1919 in the town of Weimar, the capital Berlin then being controlled by Marxists and Bolshevists.

recently elected head Adolf Hitler and his SA. Hitler readily accepted this opportunity to show the vitality of the Movement. The Bavarian SA had meanwhile increased from six to fourteen companies, each of 100 men.

Transport for these personnel was quickly planned and organized with flags and a military band of forty-two musicians to arrive punctually by special train. Scarcely had they alighted at Coburg than they were accosted by a crowd of thousands of Communists who received them with shouts of 'Bandits!' 'Thieves!' 'Criminals!', that selfsame vocabulary employed even today by respectable historians when referring to the SA. Reaction was disciplined – the orders were to avoid being provoked during the march through the town to previously arranged quarters (a field with tents) – even though the streets were thronged with great masses of Marxists whose vocabulary was ingenious. Once the vituperation was replaced by stoning, the commanders of the SA legions went on the defensive and the fighting lasted all night with injuries suffered by both sides. This was an encounter similar to that of 16 August in Munich when staves and paving stones had been used.

During the return to the station next day there was hand-to-hand fighting but again the SA emerged victorious. Its 1,400 street fighters arrived in the 'Capital of the Movement' as Munich was later known in National Socialist terminology, fortified in their sense of comradeship and personal pride. For the first time the incipient SA had made its mark on the Marxist organizations in their 'class struggle' on the streets. *'Die Strasse frei! Den braunen Bataillonen! Die Strasse frei! Dem Sturm-abteilungsmann!'** were the opening lines of the 'Horst Wessel' hymn, second verse, which appeared later. It used an old melody, but the lyrics which would be sung by countless millions in the Third Reich had yet to be written. There was also no sign yet of the brown uniforms – not until January

---

* Free translation: 'Clear the street for the brown battalions! Clear the street for the SA-Man!'

1923, when 6,000 men paraded at a Party rally for the consecration of their standards were they worn for the first time. Until that day an SA man dressed to suit himself and was distinguished from the ordinary population only by the swastika armband: now the hearts of National Socialists beat within similar unforms. The political army of 100,000 men envisioned by Hitler had begun to march.

On the other side of the Austrian Alps – was it really a coincidence? – a few hundred kilometres south, another political movement marched in synchrony with the militant rise of the SA on 'German Day' at Coburg. 28 October 1922 was the day when Mussolini marched on Rome with his 'Blackshirts'. This marked the birth of Fascism. Scarcely fourteen days later the King of Italy commissioned the leader of the march and his movement to form a new government. Mussolini acceded to power much more rapidly than Hitler and remained leader for twenty-one years compared to Hitler's twelve. His death was no less horrible. The last member of the gang which murdered Mussolini and his concubine during their attempted escape to Switzerland, a Michele Noretti, died at age 86 in a Como asylum taking with him to the grave the identity of the shooter and who was responsible for the aberrant act which followed, hanging the two corpses head down at a Milan service station.

Hitler and Mussolini had never met at the time when the former was marching through Coburg and the other to Rome; most probably the Italian leader was not even aware of Hitler's existence. Hitler, however, knew of the future Duce and already admired him. He enthused not only over the exhortations of the Italian leader: '*Credere! Obbedire! Combattere!*' ('Believe! Obey! Fight!') which had transformed him from a convinced socialist into a passionate nationalist during the fighting of the Great War – Mussolini had been seriously wounded on the River Isonzo – but also the courageous way in which the Italian leader had taken his country's destiny into his own hands (although unfortunately history was to prove those hands not so strong as first appeared).

Certainly the first successes of the Duce were achieved under much more favourable conditions than those with which the Germans had to cope. Italy had not just lost a war nor been forced to labour under the burden of a 'Dictate of Versailles' whose provisions were impossible to accommodate even for a people as disciplined and devoted to work as the Germans. After Mussolini was ousted, Italy abandoned its original ally just as it had done in the First World War, preferring to side with the common enemy of the beginning. This attitude may be interpreted in whatever way one wishes, but the Allies viewed it differently second time round. After the Great War, Italy was gifted the South Tyrol; after the second Italy was stripped of all its colonies and diverse small territories and islands in Yugoslavia, Greece and France. At least it suffered no dis-memberment into four parts as did Germany, robbed of a quarter of its natural territory, losing fifteen million Germans in the process (of whom three million were brutally murdered), bombed to rubble like no other nation and worst of all, deprived of its national identity.

For German soldiers who returned in 1918 to their sick homeland, the war was not over. On all German borders, but particularly in the Baltic and Silesia (today annexed and occupied by Poland), the armed enemy set out to add to those territories it had already handed to itself by the Dictate of Versailles. The 'hyenas' who made these incursions into Germany had to be repelled by whatever weapons remained in the hands of the Freikorps and other groups of civilian defenders. In the interior, the working masses – instigated and poisoned by the Bolshevists, especially in the main factory centres of Munich, the Ruhr, Saxony, Hamburg, Berlin and other large cities – had to be reined back and reintegrated within the disordered country in a regimented process. Germany, defeated not at the fronts but from within, needed weapons and soldiers. It was therefore logical that armed groups should spring up like mushrooms after the storm.

It was not 'the continuation of the warlike tradition inculcated in the trenches' as is expressed sarcastically by the up-and-coming generations of Longerich historians or, even worse, those such as the American writer Goldhagen who think that 'the German has in his genes the obsession to kill', yet how easy it is for them to understand 'self-defence' when it occurs in their own backyard! There is nowadays a popular but wrong opinion that the Germany of 1918 was not kept alive by the Weimar Republic, but the Freikorps who despised the Republic, its colours of black-red-gold and its representatives. Adolf Hitler observed rightly in *Mein Kampf* that it was the Freikorps, formed almost in their totality from soldiers to whom Germany continued to be important, who saved the Republic from the governing regimes installed by the Red revolution of 1918. The Freikorps risked their necks for the sake of a country raped by Marxism. There were few who, like Hitler, had clear vision.

The SA leaders Klintzsch, Göring, Röhm and others had been career officers and thought like the military class. They wanted to make the SA a paramilitary organization. Hitler was merely a senior private, but his political inclination and talents were extraordinary enough to be recognized openly by his superiors. For Hitler, the SA would no longer be an organization for civilian defence, a competitor to others in existence, but a factor for disciplined order and morale based on the ethical principles of Prussian militarism. His philosophy was something totally new, a symbiosis of politics and military discipline. The Party's 'Assault Brigade', the SA, baptized as such after the Hofbräuhaus brawls, was to exist not primarily to fight and clash and confront, but rather to be the 'town crier' for the programme. Only in the case of necessity was it to defend against the violence of its unscrupulous adversaries.*

Its founder also intended that the 'demilitarized' SA would be no more than an integral branch or sector of the Movement. Under Röhm, in the period of its spectacular growth, the SA began to develop a life of its own, assimilating aims alien to those of Hitler. For the present the differences were not aired in public but both sides adhered to their respective viewpoints without budging an inch. The final decision was postponed for years, and would have its tragic outcome in the events of 30 June 1934 with the death of Röhm and other SA commanders, a political stroke perhaps unique in the history of any country anywhere.

In the early 1920s on the other side of the Alps the example of Mussolini and his Blackshirts was awakening the interest of all Germans concerned for the future of their country, bound as it was by the restraints of Versailles. The Duce had realized that the international socialism yearned for by so many, and which Karl Marx had thought could be achieved, would never succeed in practice, that it was utopian, an intellectual mind game. The former editor of the socialist magazine *Avanti* was also convinced that true socialism could only be achieved within national borders, within a more or less homogenous mass of the people. This was the ideological base upon which Mussolini formed his Fascist movement and which, despite logical differences originating within the national character, influenced the formation of National Socialism in Germany.

Adolf Hitler, admirer of the Duce, shared in principle Mussolini's political–military point of view. The Blackshirts were never intended to supplant the Italian Army, nor even complement it, although the Fascist militia was subordinated later within the regular Army. The initial idea was that like the

* Hitler, *Mein Kampf*, p. 601.

SA it should be the 'battering ram' of the political movement, and its rapid success proved that the concept was right. Hitler realized this immediately and drew his own conclusions. The march to the Feldherrnhalle in Munich, held a short while later in November 1923, cost sixteen NSDAP men and four police-men their lives. The incident was exalted and almost glorified by National Socialism, yet it had been under the military control of Ludendorff, not the political control of Hitler. Both were marching at the head of the demonstration when government troops opened fire, causing deaths and injuries, but these two leaders escaped unharmed. When, as a result of this attempted coup, the NSDAP and SA were proscribed, Röhm and Ludendorff entered the Reichstag as deputies of the Deutschvölkische Freiheitspartei, enjoying its expenses and allowances while Hitler, Hess and others were sentenced to imprisonment. A little later Röhm returned to Bolivia to take up a post as military adviser. Ludendorff stood as a candidate for the Presidency in 1925, but only 1.1 per cent of the electorate voted for him. He then devoted himself to editing a fortnightly magazine, the journal of the Tannenbergbund which he had founded himself, and to writing for various political and military satirical magazines.

The differences between Hitler and Röhm as to whether the SA should be primarily political or military in nature continued and the gulf between them never narrowed. The rift was not even discussed privately; it remained unspoken. Even after he was elected head of the NSDAP on 29 July 1921, Adolf Hitler continued to insist that the SA had to be a political body bound to the Party, and not an independent institution.

The otherwise praiseworthy historian and former SA General, Heinrich Bennecke, is mistaken when he states in his book on the Reich and Röhm insurrection that 'Hitler had considered from the outset the creation of a National Socialist Army drawn from the SA and organized at the beginning for

other purposes'* and ex-Gauleiter Rudolf Jordan is even wider
of the mark when in his support of Bennecke he alleges that
'any recent revolution could be sure of success if it created a
new Army from within its own ranks', and as an example he
quotes Trotsky. Adolf Hitler never planned to seize power
violently, only legally. He said so unequivocally in *Mein Kampf*
which he wrote in Landsberg Prison where he was confined
following the failed revolt of 9 November 1923.

The waters of his relationship with the Reichswehr of the
Weimar Republic, which he supported from the outset and
which was the source of his income, became muddied when on
1 March 1923 he had to give back the weapons which he and
his supporters had received at the time when the Marxist
revolution was feared. There was no chance of a peaceful
revolution with Ludendorff, which he knew from 8 November
1923. Hitler chose the legal path to power. This path would be
long and thorny. Already during the proceedings in the Bavarian
People's Courts (26 February–1 April 1924) and later, during
the Reichswehr trials at Ulm against three young National
Socialist officers, Hitler had committed himself formally to
pursue his aim of seizing power in Germany only by con-
stitutional means, and he kept his word. Once in power, the
armaments of the Reich were not then passed out again to
Röhm and the SA which he led, but kept in the Reichswehr
arsenals, and when, following the death of Reich President von
Hindenburg on 2 August 1934, the armed forces were placed
under the command of the 'Führer and Reich Chancellor', they
swore to him personally their oath of allegiance.

* Heinrich Bennecke, *Die Reichswehr und der Röhm-Putsch*,
Munich/Vienna, 1964.

CHAPTER 7

Röhm in a Tight Spot

There is no doubt that Röhm was homosexual. This became known after his court case in Berlin in 1925, but in public his orientation remained only a rumour. 'I think I am homosexual,' he admitted to his spiritual confessor Dr Heimsoth, a Berlin medical practitioner, in a letter from Bolivia on 25 February 1929, and added: 'I discovered it for certain in 1924. Previously I had had relationships with many women, although never with special pleasure. Today women disgust me, particularly those who pursue me with great love.' He finished off by observing: 'And lamentably there are many of them.'

Röhm's deviation from the natural sexual instinct came out – according to his own admission – in 1924. Taking into account that he was born on 28 November 1887, it took him until he was 37 to discover these tendencies, that is to say, until he was a mature man. When later the *Münchener Post* published some undoubted documents in proof, the letters to the Berlin doctor of 22 June 1931 and May the following year, his homosexuality was confirmed. The former Reichstag Deputy Dr Helmut Klotz made available the letters during an arraignment in 1932 for a contravention of Article 175 of the Civil Code (Illegality of Homosexual Acts) which Röhm admitted.* In the letter of 25 February 1929 from La Paz, when he was serving as a colonel in the Bolivian Army, he wrote: 'I do not feel unfortunate to have these sexual preferences, although they often cause me annoying problems.

---

* Dr Helmut Klotz, *Der Fall Röhm*, Berlin, 1932.

But psychologically I have no remorse, on the contrary I almost feel proud of it.'

The 'pride' can be inferred from another letter dated 3 December 1928, written by hand to the same addressee in which he complained of the sniping by the 'moral athlete' Alfred Rosenberg against him; he attributed these acid criticisms to 'my not having made any secret of my inclinations', adding that in National Socialist circles the people 'will have to get used to it'. This was not the right way to go about things, and in the face of increasing open criticism, Röhm was forced to institute proceedings 'for the suffering caused him by the publication of his letters' since their authenticity had been confirmed in a previous trial.

Supreme Federal Attorney Dr Klemmer, who had headed the investigations against Röhm for the Article 175 offence, revealed that he had shown the three letters in question to Röhm for authentication, and Röhm had confirmed that he had written, edited and signed them. The Article 175 trial did not result in a conviction, however.

Apart from it dawning upon him that year that he was homosexual, 1924 was also an important year for Röhm in another respect: it was the year he entered the Reichstag for the first time, at the start of the second parliament period beginning on 4 May. His party, the NSDAP was proscribed and its leader in Landsberg Prison, although he would be released in the coming December. Röhm consoled himself by joining the Deutschvölkische Freiheitspartei, which had obtained 6.5 per cent of the votes, entitling it to 32 of the 472 seats in the Reichstag. Another of the deputies who entered the parliament in the same way was Erich Ludendorff (1865–1937). Of the 32, 11 were nationalists like Röhm and included names well-known even today such as Gottfried Feder (1883–1941), one of the founders of the NSDAP and author of its manifesto, and Wilhelm Frick (1877–1946) the first Interior Minister of the Third Reich.

Nominated as a candidate but not elected was Roland Freisler (1893–1945), a former Communist and later President of the People's Court in the Third Reich. A little-known biographical detail about this man was revealed by the Social Democrat magazine *Vorwärts* in its edition of 3 May 1924 under the title 'Spiritual Kinship; Jewish-Communist, Popular German Reichstag Candidate'. This same Dr Roland Freisler, who originated from Kassel, had been until rather recently a member of the German Communist Party, and the official organ of the Social Democrats added that this detail was all the more interesting because 'his grandmother was a full Jewess (as in the case of Wulle)'. Uncovering this detail from within a mountain of material relating to the history of the SA, and having published it first, is one of the many successes of the historian Georg Franz-Willing, mentioned elsewhere. Freisler, the losing candidate suggested by Ludendorff in 1924, managed to be elected to the Reichstag in 1932 after having joined the NSDAP in 1925 when the ban was lifted. He died in the cellars of the People's Court in February 1945 during one of the countless Allied air raids on Berlin.

Former Army captain and now Reichstag deputy Ernst Röhm enjoyed from 1924 those benefits which were available to a democratically elected representative of the people in the Weimar Republic. He collected many expenses, travelled the length and breadth of Germany first class by train and enjoyed himself in Berlin by night. Also in the year when he finished his term as a Reichstag deputy and had accepted the Bolivian offer to be a military adviser in La Paz, he recalled in one of the last letters he wrote to Dr Heimsoth the glorious days he had had the fortune to experience in Berlin as a representative of the people. He recalled that beautiful city with nostalgia. What had enchanted him most there were the Turkish baths, 'the peak of human pleasure'. It was precisely there that he enjoyed in a special way 'the pleasure of personal relations'. In that 'delightful metropolis' of which Röhm had such nostalgic memories in his letter of homosexual regrets, he enjoyed what were cynically described as the 'golden years of the twenties'. For those who, like us, were joined under the sign of the swastika, the times were anything but 'golden'. Turkish baths and other pleasures were unknown to us. We should like to have sweated, not to lose a few kilos before the boys pampered us, but from hard toil instead of forming queues for the dole. Of the unnatural pleasures enjoyed by Herr Röhm we still knew nothing; the talk would come later. Some of the revelations came to light in 1932 from Dr Klotz's book[*] and then after Röhm's 'insurrection' all the world knew. Röhm's aversion to women seemed to intensify during his period in the Reichstag. In his book he confessed his satisfaction that his party had been the only one for which no women had been named as candidates and added bitterly that the motto *mulier taceat* (the female should remain quiet)[†] could not be bettered. The women of today, he assured his readers,[‡] were in all things the men who subjected themselves to women. It was difficult to imagine that such men as Alexander the Great, Frederick the Great or Caesar, Napoleon, Prince Eugene of Savoy or Charles XII of Sweden would have been submissive to a woman. One notices from this crafty list of soldiers of world history an absentee: Erich Ludendorff, master of logistics in the German Army; the man who, from 1916 was Röhm's supreme commander and who had shared, together with Hindenburg, the fame of defeating the Russians at Tannenberg in East Prussia.

Originally Röhm admired him unconditionally, but began to be critical in the 1920s when Ludendorff gradually succumbed to the influence of his second wife, Mathilde Spiess von

[*] Klotz, *Der Fall Röhm*.
[†] First Corinthians, 14:34.
[‡] Röhm, *Geschichte eines Hochverräters*.

Kemnitz, whom he had married once his first wife, interned in a mental asylum, no longer presented a legal obstacle. The ambitious Frau von Kemnitz conquered her heroic husband in such a way that she was the one who gave the orders in the home. This embittered Röhm very much.

During his four-year term in the Reichstag he had kept his seat warm, having risen to speak on just the one occasion, a triviality. The question was now, what to do next? The Reichswehr would not have him because of the treason conviction which had earned him fifteen months' imprisonment in 1923, (even though he was granted early release in 1924). To support himself he at first sold books for a female publisher, was employed by a commercial firm and finally the 1924 elections plucked him out of his precarious situation. His military interests extended to the creation of a Frontbann, a kind of civilian defence organization of which there were numerous examples in Bavaria, and to which he supplied arms. He also attempted to supply weapons to the SA, but Hitler intervened. After his own release from Landsberg at the end of 1924 and the lifting of the ban on the NSDAP and SA, Hitler was not interested in 'playing at soldiers'.

On 25 February 1925 the Weimar Republic cancelled the decree banning both institutions and next day the Party newspaper *Völkischer Beobachter* published Hitler's directives for the re-forming of the Movement and its various organizations. The SA was only restructured along the general lines pertaining before the ban. 'The purpose of the SA', Hitler said, 'is to strengthen our youth physically, educate them to value healthy ideals and discipline, and spread the principles of our Movement.' These guidelines were clear and simple. Hitler wanted the SA only for protection at his meetings and to support the new political movement. This was contrary to what Röhm intended with his Frontbann to which, apparently, Ludendorff had also lent his support.

Hitler had entrusted the leadership of the SA to Röhm temporarily during the ban because Göring, who had inherited it from the youthful Oberleutnant zur See Klintzsch, had been seriously wounded during the shoot-out at the Feldherrnhalle and been forced to flee to Austria and then Sweden, his wife's country of origin, to escape arrest. Röhm now wanted to incorporate the re-born SA into his Frontbann. Hitler would not allow this and, lacking his approval, Röhm's Frontbann was stillborn, and he had no choice but to abandon the idea.

At this point one can see the barrier which separated Hitler and Röhm after the failure of 9 November 1923, and the *Völkischer Beobachter* article mentioned above leaves no doubt: 'Armed groups are excluded from the SA. Whoever carries a weapon in contravention of the directive of the leadership, or stocks weapons, will be expelled immediately from both the SA and the NSDAP.'[*]

In a circular dated 26 May 1925 there appeared clear and unequivocal confirmation that 'Herr Hitler is not thinking of organizing an armed political movement. If he did so at any time in the past, it was only under pressure from people who later abandoned him. Today the only thing Hitler needs is a guard to protect his closed meetings as prior to 1923.' Everybody knew whom the circular meant by the word 'people': not Röhm, who despite his officer's rank had sub-ordinated himself discreetly to Hitler, but the police authority of the state of Bavaria, Kahr and Ludendorff, each of whom in 1923 had his own private agenda.

For my part, I can confirm in good faith as a person who served in the ranks of the SA, the non-military character of the organization. In the entire year of my service as a volunteer I never participated in a single military manoeuvre. Admittedly we wore uniform and marched in step and came to attention when ordered to do so, but more important for us than the

[*] Heinrich Bennecke, 'Neubildung der SA', *Völkischer Beobachter*, 26 February 1925.

physical exercises was the ideological instruction. Nobody had reason to teach us weapons drill as almost all had served at the front in the Great War.

Röhm saw no future for himself after leaving the Reichstag and the Turkish baths; his attempts to fit into civilian life did not go well. It was then that he remembered an offer received in 1926 to join a military mission in Bolivia, a subject which had not interested him while he sat in the Reichstag. In 1911 my country of birth had exchanged a French military mission for a German one. In 1926, when under the presidency of the pro-German Hernando Siles (1883–1942), relations with neighbouring Paraguay had become very difficult over the disputed Chaco region, Bolivia attempted to improve the efficiency of its army by having its troops trained by German instructors. For this purpose, German General Hans Kundt (1869–1939) came to Bolivia after many years of active service to take up the post of Chief of the Bolivian General Staff, and once installed his attention was drawn to Hauptmann Röhm, organizer of the civilian defenders of Bavaria. I might mention in passing that Kundt was a member of my parents' circle of friends. His name was familiar to me from what my mother told me about him and he enjoyed a good relationship within La Paz social and political circles. It was Kundt who, at the end of 1928, gave Röhm his contract to come to Bolivia as an instructor and training officer for the military.

Within twenty-four hours Röhm had accepted the offer, certainly a tempting one in his current circumstances. He had had to resign his commission five years before and had found only a poor recompense in the paramilitary civilian defence organizations. Thus the Bolivian job came as manna from heaven. Kundt promised him a rank equivalent to lieutenant colonel in the General Staff, which was two grades higher than he had had with the Reichswehr. Three days later he embarked for passage first class aboard the German transatlantic liner *Cap*

Polonia, and disembarked at Buenos Aires. Apparently Röhm felt very much at home in La Paz at 3,669 metres above sea level, my birthplace sixteen years before. He felt joy and contentment to be there because 'this world does not see the Germany of November 1918, does not have prejudices as such, but believes in its old honourable traditions and in the fresh force of the new Germany', he wrote in one of his letters. Röhm required six months to acclimatize and gain a working knowledge of the language, and then the moment came when Kundt could use him as an instructor to lead two infantry regiments where, with his talent for organization, he had the opportunity to apply his military skill and the Prussian virtues. 'Here I could be a soldier heart and soul,' he confessed in his memoirs. 'In optimum collaboration with the regimental commanders I was able to demand high performance which was achieved efficiently and with goodwill' he wrote, and in fact his work in the Altiplano was so satisfactory that he was made chief of staff of an army division.

Röhm never regretted his time as an officer in Bolivia, despite the political revolution in that country causing him more than one personal problem. The 1930 revolution was one of the routine coups which occur regularly in Latin American republics, always instigated and conducted by foreign interests, and usually involving the nearest neighbour as an enemy. President Siles was not to the taste of the foreign puppeteers who managed South American politics. His friend General Kundt attempted to protect him but the opposition was too strong. Kundt was forced to seek sanctuary in the German diplomatic mission, which succeeded in getting him repatriated.

In 1930 Röhm also sensed the anti-German animosity of the revolution. Calm soon returned following the military coup and another civilian administration was inserted in place of Siles, but Röhm still did not feel comfortable with it.

Meanwhile he could see how the situation in Germany was deteriorating daily. The crash of the New York Stock Exchange of 25 October 1929 sparked off a world economic crisis which punished Germany especially hard, coming so soon after the hyperinflation of 1923 had been overcome by stabilizing the Reichsmark. The wave of industrial, commercial and banking bankruptcies set off uncontrollable unemployment at a time when the public finances were falling into a bottomless pit. The Berlin banking and export company of which my father had once headed the La Paz branch, where I had learned the profession of banker, folded, and I became one of the more than six million unemployed who wandered the streets of Germany.

Heinrich Brüning, the Catholic Centre Party politician who attempted to govern by decree from May 1930, was unable to halt the economic and political collapse in Germany. In this desperate situation elections were held on 14 September 1930. They were a true landslide. The number of seats won by the National Socialists rose spectacularly from twelve to 107. This converted the NSDAP into the second largest party after the Social Democrats who, like all the other political parties apart from the Communists, sustained huge losses. Other than the Nazis the only other party actually to gain seats was the KPD (Communist Party). Their share rose from 54 to 77, a gain of 23, which made them the third largest group in the Reichstag. This was the red light for Germany. Our swastika flag was red and so was the Communist banner; this gave middle-class 'democrats' a terrible shock. Between the two flags the only difference was that ours had the swastika and theirs the hammer and sickle.

In that European autumn, Germany had reached the verge of decisive change. Hitler now had to assemble all available forces to achieve his goal. The SA must play a preponderant role, of that he was convinced. Who could lead it most efficiently? His thoughts wandered to distant Bolivia. And what happened next Röhm expressed in his book in this way: 'Then came a telephone call from my friend Hitler.' The voice was penetrating and laconic. 'I need you', it said.

CHAPTER 8

Riding a Horse Unaided

Adolf Hitler had good reason to summon his old friend with such urgency. The electoral earthquake of September 1930 occasioned a radical change in the political landscape of Germany on a scale which nobody can have foreseen, not even Hitler himself. To achieve second place in the voting was not in itself sensational, by to do so by an increase in the share of the seats from twelve to 107 was unique in German parliamentary history. For the absolute majority needed to take power legally, as Hitler had promised, there was still a long way to go. The second runners-up were the Communists, who had increased their tally of seats from 23 to 77, and it would require a great effort to reverse this trend in the struggle to win power. Hitler knew that the SA would be indispensable, as strong and as disciplined as possible. Who better than Röhm to handle it? Hitler was aware of Röhm's homosexuality as the result of complaints from indignant Party members, but he valued Röhm's leadership qualities so highly that he waved aside the accusations with the argument that the allegations were unproven.

The sensational fact that a political party, scarcely five years after its rehabilitation, could increase its potential tenfold was a powerful indication that absolute power was attainable. Its political successes were already visible at the local and provincial government levels as well as in the executive and legislature. The province of Brunswick had a Nationalist as Minister of the Interior, Dietrich Klagges (from 1933 Prime

Minister of this province). He appointed Adolf Hitler, then an Austrian national, to his ministry as an adviser, which automatically conferred upon him German citizenship. Until then, 25 February 1932, the leader of the German Nazi Party was not German! In March 1932 Hitler was thus able to present his candidacy for the Reich presidency in competition with the sitting President von Hindenburg, and the Communist leader Ernst Thälmann. He obtained 11.34 million votes against the Communist's 4.5 million. Hindenburg won with 18.65 million votes. The race for power was not limited to the elections; it was more important to win and hold the streets. Until this moment the Communists believed they controlled the asphalt. No challenge to them was possible without an efficient strong-arm SA.

Within the SA things had not been working well. Fifteen days before the elections of 14 March the 'Stennes Revolt' had begun to boil in the ranks. It was the first serious crisis which Dr Goebbels had had to face in Berlin. He often spoke to me of it during the two years I spent with him and his family, in his home and office.

The first person with whom Goebbels discussed the matter was Göring, who was later to play an important role in the events of 30 June 1934. In his diary entry for 24 August 1930 Goebbels wrote of the previous afternoon. 'Dinner with Göring. Serious conversation about the SA ... it is becoming too independent under Stennes and Pfeffer ... personally am ever less trusting of Stennes.' His fears were justified. A week later the rumours about a revolt within the Berlin SA were confirmed. 'Stennes is arranging the threads like a spider in its web' he wrote in his diary on 30 August 1930. The move was even more grave than he thought. 'Stennes is a traitor'.*

Both faced off openly. The head of SA-East, as SA Berlin-Brandenburg was known, put his uncomplicated demands on

---

* *Die Tagebücher von Joseph Goebbels*, Munich & New York, 1987.

the table: three Reichstag seats for the SA, money and participation in the political decisions of the Movement. Should these demands not be met, the big demonstration which Goebbels was preparing for the next day in the Palace of Sport and aimed at the coming elections would be ruined by force. Goebbels attempted to calm the rebel: he would speak to Hitler to get him to take into account the justified claims of the SA. He kept his promise and scribbled in his diary, with an almost illegible note for me so that I should remember it every day: 'I am urging him to hold back until after the elections. Moreover, with regard to the subject of financing, the SA is right' (a noteworthy admission which Goebbels confirmed to me personally during the last months we were together).

At that time, most SA men lived a really miserable existence. Amongst themselves they discussed openly if it was fair that in Munich they were spending millions building the Braunes Haus HQ, while those in Berlin did not know where the money was coming from to sole and heel their worn-down boots for the next Party march. To this was added the fact that although the SA was a body with independent leaders, it was the Party which had the last word in all political decisions including those relating to SA internal organization. This unscrupulous attitude towards the SA was not only manifest in the financial methods of the Party, but also in the nomination of candidates for the various parliaments and guilds. The SA felt itself treated contemptuously within the Movement, the Cinderella of the National Socialist family. As Goebbels knew, it was not done deliberately. The Berlin Gauleiter was implicated to some extent in all the Party revolts – that of Stennes in 1930 was certainly not the only one – and he might have been involved in stirring this one too. Goebbels represented what was considered the 'Left wing' of the Party, for whom the 'National' was the unchallenged basis for all political activity and the 'Socialist' was the revolutionary factor of the

Movement, born from the disaster of the Great War, and which could not be renounced.

On 30 August 1930 Stennes 'struck' in the true sense of the word: the Party offices of the Berlin section on Hedemann-Strasse were totally wrecked. The police had to intervene. Blood flowed, 'family blood' as Goebbels observed in his dairy. The SS men who got involved sustained injuries. Gauleiter Goebbels was ⌐a a propaganda tour in Breslau, capital of Silesia, and was informed of the occurrence at two in the morning. He dropped everything, notified Hitler, and both travelled immediately to Berlin. 'Things are on a knife edge,' Goebbels noted. He struggled to find a peaceful solution until Hitler confronted Stennes. 'Stennes gave in,' Goebbels wrote.

The Supreme SA-Führer, Pfeffer von Salomon, a former Army captain as had been Stennes and Röhm, resigned. The economic problems of the Berlin SA were settled to the satisfaction of all. In the social centre of the Kriegerverein (War Veterans' Club), the traditional venue of Party meetings, the SA leaders and men assembled. Hitler was accompanied by one of the most respected personalities of the Party, Karl Litzmann, a general who wore the Pour le Mérite. His 3rd Infantry Division had gone through the enemy lines at Brzeziny in Poland. A couple of decades later, aged eighty, he enjoyed great esteem and respect. Hitler and Litzmann spoke with the SA. Initially there was a frosty response, but at the end the men broke out in deafening applause and oaths of loyalty. Now nothing could prevent the great electoral success that was to follow two weeks later.

I describe the Stennes Revolt here in perhaps rather more than the usual detail because it was very important for my personal future and not only politically. I came into contact with Stennes through a Party member, Günter Heysing, a dyed-in-the-wool Berliner from the Wedding district, the working-class heart of the Reich capital. He was also a journalist, a few years older than I, but educated in totally different circles to mine. He spoke the Berlin dialect which I, arrived from Silesia a few years before, could never have imitated. His great love was militarism. Long before the Third Reich, and also long before the reintroduction of conscription, he had volunteered for the Reichswehr infantry, which still retained at that time the military brilliance of the old traditions which its veterans passed on much later to the Waffen-SS. He rose rapidly through the ranks to captain while I never made it past lieutenant. He was one of the few war correspondents to be awarded the Iron Cross First Class. Together we formed part of the Berichter-staffel des OKH (Army High Command Propaganda Company) in the General Staff.

Heysing taught me the basics and aims of National Socialism long before I joined the SA in 1931, then the only institution where people of our age could develop their ideological thinking. All I lacked to draw me into the Movement after this theoretical and intellectual indoctrination were the truncheon blows to the back of the head kindly administered by the police 'defenders of democracy', and already well known to Heysing, Goebbels, 'Auwi' and many others. I have no idea if Stennes was given the same pasting as we were. His biography, written by a former Royal Navy officer and chief of the British secret service during the war, was published in Germany in 1982 under the title *When Hitler went to Canossa*.* How did Hitler get to Canossa? The encyclopaedia tells us: 'Canossa, fortress and castle at Emilia, Italy. Henry IV, Emperor of the West, was humiliated there by Pope Gregory VII during the Investiture Crisis (1077), being made to wait for days until the Pope released him from excommunication.' As a German idiomatic expression, 'Canossa' was made into a slogan when Bismarck told the Reichstag on 18 March 1872 'We shall not go to Canossa' and kept his word. Hitler did not detour to Canossa

---

* German version, Charles Drage, *Als Hitler nach Canossa ging*, 1982.

when he hurried to Berlin on 31 August 1930. He did not go there to absolve himself of blame or beg forgiveness, but to reason with an angry membership.

The talk had a result. In his long and varied military career, Hauptmann Walter Stennes (1895–1981) laboured under the nickname 'SI' – 'Uneasy Subordinate'. And he was. At age ten he was a cadet at Bensberg/Rhine; during the First World War he became a lieutenant and was decorated. Much later he created the Freikorps *Hacketau* which fought the incursions on the Polish front postwar. In 1920 he took part in the Kapp coup, spent a brief period in the 'green' police – green for the colour of their uniforms – and later in the 'black Reichswehr', and finally joined the 'brown SA' in 1927, turning it little by little into an 'Uneasy Subordinate' institution like himself. If his British biographer is to be believed, Stennes met Hitler in 1920 at the Berlin residence of Graf Ernst zu Reventlow (1869–1943), a Holstein aristocrat who later headed the extreme right wing of the NSDAP. These 'Pan-Germans' held their meetings in his hospitable mansion where fruitful political conversations ensued. Adolf Hitler – his name was known in Berlin in connection with his political movement, whose tendencies were then not known as accurately – was frequently discussed. Despite his Austro-Bavarian origins, Hitler achieved an excellent rapport with the former naval officer from the north coast. Reventlow joined the NSDAP in 1927 and argued its ideology with great dignity during the period of the ban and as a Reichstag deputy in Ludendorff's party. In this he was certainly better than Röhm, his parliamentary colleague. One day Gräfin Reventlow told the young Stennes – one of her guests – that her husband was currently speaking with an amazing political figure from Munich, whom many people from there considered to be the 'new Messiah'. Author Drage confirms reports that Stennes heard this and said, 'this guy does not resemble a Messiah, not even a false one'.

The same year, Ludendorff introduced Stennes to Hitler, and before the failed coup of November 1923 Hitler presumably offered Stennes the leadership of an SA formation. This never came about, apparently, because Stennes was busy as a Reichswehr training instructor, where he considered himself indispensable. Shortly after the re-creation of the NSDAP in 1925, Stennes resumed contact with the unquestioned leader of the Party through his protector Ludendorff, but he waited until the spring of 1927 before accepting a position that suited him, leader of SA-East, which covered the whole region of Central Germany to the Elbe, including the capital Berlin. With this he was happy. From December 1927 one of the five SA districts covering the German Reich, and by far the most important, was controlled by Stennes.

In the Berlin district, Goebbels managed the political affairs of the Party. From amongst all those highly placed in the political administration it was Stennes who gave him the most recognition and support, according to his British biographer. Hitler was not the expected Messiah for Stennes, but a man like everybody else, with whom he got on well. He considered that Frick had the average capabilities of a Bavarian public employee. He put Hess in the category of 'Parsifal, the loyal follower' (Hess remained his sworn enemy to the end). Of only one of the front-line personalities did he speak well: his superior in the political sphere, Joseph Goebbels. He was 'simply extraordinary' and by far 'the most intelligent of them all'. Stennes described the most outstanding characteristics of the future Minister of Propaganda as being, for example, 'a real pleasure to hear him speak, he was always convincing. He was an excellent musician and a first-class story teller. He had the most expressive hands and eyes I ever saw in my life.'[*]

---

[*] Wilfred von Oven, *Mit Goebbels bis zum Ende*, Buenos Aires 1948/ 1949, latest edition, Bingen, 1995, under the title, *Dr Goebbels – Meister der Propaganda*.

I can confirm personally word for word what Stennes said; after all I shared the life of Goebbels and his family for two years. While Stennes took advantage of his elevated position within the growing NSDAP to prepare and bring about internal insurrection, the SA was transforming itself – after its rebirth in 1925, under the general command of former Hauptmann Franz Felix Pfeffer von Salomon, and the precise directive of Adolf Hitler – into an important, if not decisive instrument of the Movement. 'Pfeffer', a distant relation of the famed author Ernst von Salomon, was born at Düsseldorf in 1888 and entered the Army as a cadet in 1907. He was a Korpsstudent – a member of a students' duelling corps. During the First World War he became a battalion commander and attained the rank of captain. After 1918 he founded and led his West-fälisches Freikorps *Pfeffer* against the Bolshevists in the Baltic region and Silesia, later participated in the Kapp putsch of 1920 and fought the French and Belgian invaders who occupied the Ruhr on 11 January 1923. This led to his arrest and trial by a French military tribunal. He managed to escape the sentence of death suffered by his Freikorps colleague Albert Leo Schlageter.

Pfeffer von Salomon joined the NSDAP as Member 16,101 as soon as it became newly legal in 1925 and was nominated Gauleiter for Westphalia. This did not amount to much since the few Party members there had little say. During 1925 the local government in Westphalia was expanded into the Greater Ruhr region which embraced a huge human resource. For this reason it was decided to form an executive triumvirate consisting of Pfeffer and two personalities of great importance later: Goebbels and Karl Kaufmann (1900–69), Gauleiter of Hamburg. On 1 November 1926 Pfeffer was happy to accept Hitler's offer of the post of Supreme SA-Führer.

During the brief four years he was in charge of the SA, Pfeffer von Salomon injected into it its characteristic military discipline and organization. All the important posts were filled by former Freikorps men. There was an excellent understanding between them. The homogeneity of the body of commanders was what gave an organization of such meteoric growth that legendary effectiveness in its role as the stormtroop of the NSDAP.

Nevertheless, the old difference between the soldier Röhm and the politician Hitler persisted even with the SA under new command. Pfeffer had quickly demanded the introduction of principles to separate strictly the jurisdiction and duties of the SA and NSDAP. The Party activist was to be the natural propagandist of National Socialist ideology while the SA man dominated the street and provided physical defence for Party meetings and demonstrations. The antagonism which had already been responsible for friction between Hitler and Röhm continued under Pfeffer's leadership. After the Stennes Revolt in Berlin, Hitler took over leadership of the SA personally, creating an executive post of Stabschef, equivalent to SA Chief of Staff, and it struck him that the person to fill this role was Röhm in Bolivia.

The parting between Hitler and the bully Pfeffer was amicable, despite their many quarrels. The Party compensated him with a secure seat amongst the Reichstag candidates for the sixth legislative period. In this way the former Supreme SA-Führer became one of the 230 new deputies elected on 31 July 1932, which converted the NSDAP so spectacularly into the second-strongest Party in the Reichstag. Six months later Hitler was nominated Reich Chancellor.

Pfeffer von Salomon was expelled from the Party in 1941 for disobeying Hitler. Shortly before the war ended, the sexagenarian took up arms once more to defend his country as commander of one of the legendary Volkssturm units, made up of armed volunteers of all ages sworn to fight to the last. They were responsible for gestures of heroism such as have rarely been known in history. Pfeffer survived it all and died in his eighties in a Munich suburb.*

In 1930, Adolf Hitler surely believed that with Pfeffer out of his hair, with Röhm back as Stabschef and himself as Supreme SA-Führer, this would put 'Germany in the saddle' of government, an expression first used by Bismarck on 11 March 1867 to the parliament of the North German Federation, describing by this proverbial phrase his work of national unification. Adolf Hitler hoped that the second part of the Bismarck quote, 'and ride away unaided' should also become reality.

* Franz Felix von Salomon, b. 19 February 1888, Düsseldorf; d. 12 April 1968, Munich.

CHAPTER 9

The Red Front and Reaction

Not many years had passed since Bismarck had spoken certain well-chosen words to the Reichstag of the still-small Germany. The victory over France in the Franco-Prussian War of 1870–1 had unified that Germany which had been dismembered by the Congress of Vienna of 1815 into thirty-five independent principalities and four autonomous cities. Bismarck proclaimed the Second Reich on 18 January 1871 in the Palace of Versailles. King Wilhelm I of Prussia was to be Emperor, and Bismarck Chancellor.

In the interim, Karl Marx had written *Das Kapital* (first edition 1867), and in 1869 in the town of Eisenach had founded social democracy, the same 'social democracy' which barely a half century later would destroy Bismarck's work by means of the revolution of November 1918. Faced with these birth pangs of Marxism, Bismarck had confessed to the legislators on 27 March 1874: 'I fear that we shall have to eradicate it.' Evidently he was having doubts about the new Germany which he had 'put in the saddle' and had 'ridden away unaided'. Hitler was in the same position when, on the eve of the creation of the Third Reich, he was forced to face up to those events under examination here.

The Stennes Revolt, apparently resolved to everybody's satisfaction, remained alive in pockets here and there as a more or less pressing issue. During the last four months of 1930, former captain and doctor *honoris causa* Otto Wagener (1888–1971), a person on very close terms with Hitler, had taken command of the SA. His curriculum vitae and career in the Party and government of the Third Reich was atypical of the membership of the National Socialist governing body.

Though the son of a wealthy Karlsruhe manufacturer, he opted for a military career. He arrived at the front direct from the Berlin Military Academy, was decorated and held several appointments until entering the General Staff in the rank of captain. After the war he fought with the Baltic Freikorps, and as a consequence of his participation in the Kapp putsch of March 1920 spent some time in a Baden-Württemberg jail. After his release he studied at the Faculty of Economic Science, where he obtained his doctorate. Meanwhile he had also taken charge of his father's sewing-machine factory at Karlsruhe.

Wagener knew Hitler from the 1929 Nuremberg Rally to which he had been invited as a representative of industry even though not a Party member. He remedied this quickly, very soon after the first personal contact with Hitler. Hitler was so impressed with him that he made him acting successor to Pfeffer. Over the next three years he had charge of various NSDAP administrative departments, especially those dealing with economic affairs. In June 1933 he withdrew from political activity. At the outbreak of war he returned to military duty, eventually rising to the rank of Generalmajor. A prisoner of the British for seven long and difficult years,* he produced his

---

* He was appointed Reich Commissioner for the Economy on 3 May 1933, but under pressure from Göring and industry, Hitler relieved him of all state and Party offices on 12 June 1933. The real reason was lobbying (in which Wagener had no part) to make him the successor to the sitting minister, Hugenberg. Wagener remained a Reichstag deputy and SA Gruppenführer until 1938. Taken prisoner in 1944, he was convicted of a war crime by an Italian tribunal in 1947 and not released from imprisonment in Italy until 1952. Christa Schroeder, *Er war mein Chef*, Herbig, 1985/2004, fn. 45, pp. 304–5.

memoirs, published with the Yale Professor Henry A. Turner, with Turner named as author.[*]

According to Professor Turner, Wagener 'remained a loyal adept of his Führer even beyond the total defeat of the Second World War', and Turner adds that Wagener grew increasingly to consider himself the 'Guardian of the Holy Grail'. In the prologue to his book with Wagener's memoir, Turner alleges that Wagener must have conversed with Hitler on hundreds of occasions, very often alone. In 1946 Wagener wrote that 'seriously' Hitler 'probably never allowed anybody else to view so openly, repeatedly and extensively the depth of his universal genius'. If Otto Wagener had not had to give up provisional command of the SA to Ernst Röhm at the beginning of 1931, the 'brown battalions' would almost certainly have marched in another direction, and not that which led to the tragedy of 30 June 1934.

Goebbels's diary for the years 1928–30 often mentions Stennes, generally critically, or even contemptuously. The cooperation between the Party and SA left much to be desired. Now and again the word 'concern' appears in the diary: concerns about the ambitious SA-East commander; concerns for the SA itself; concern for where the Movement was headed. On 13 August 1928 he wrote: 'SA in major crisis, Stennes leaving, with him many of the directors. It is time to choose and decide: revolution or reaction.'

Eleven days later in Munich, after having made an agreement with Pfeffer and Stennes in Berlin, Goebbels noted in his diary details of his conversation with Hitler. (He refers to Hitler as 'Chief' and not 'Führer'. He did use the term much later as an occasional interpolation until it became customary; it was never decreed nor ordered.) 'I have to work at it with persistence, sometimes contrary to my own convictions. One might conclude that Pfeffer and Stennes are guerrillas, perhaps

[*] Henry A. Turner (Jr), *Hitler aus nächster Nähe*, Frankfurt/Berlin/ Vienna, 1978.

correctly. But right now we cannot have the luxury of a major crisis. I am convincing the Chief of it, contrary to my better judgement.' Goebbels confirms here in his own words what his critics reproach him for even today, and what he told me a short while before the capitulation, that in every Party crisis and revolt he was always on the side of the revolutionaries, at least half-heartedly (the other half of his heart was always for Hitler). On 14 September 1928 with respect to the Stennes insurrection, he wrote: 'We want to work together loyally ... Stennes a basically good man,' and on 6 December: 'Stennes is co-operating again with enthusiasm.'

All these internal Party disputes were not so much about parliamentary business, money or influence but increasingly the question of where the National Socialist movement, and with it Germany, was headed: revolution or reaction? The question preoccupied us all. Horst Wessel, the man whom Goebbels elevated, quite intentionally, to an heroic SA figure, made it the central theme of his sensational speech at age 21, scarcely beyond his majority, at Berlin-Friedenau. Goebbels wrote animatedly on 16 January 1929: 'I heard the speech against reaction by the young member Wessel. A good lad who speaks with marvellous idealism.' A few months later, at Dresden on 30 April 1929: 'They will see how I keep our line straight. There will be no way they can label us reactionaries. I will apply all legal means possible to avoid it. We are revolutionaries and will continue to be so.'

This amounted to a declaration of war on the tendency within the Nazi Party, principally led by Göring, to canvas support from influential financial and military circles of the conservative Right, as even Hitler himself was preparing to do in order to obtain votes to assist him in his rise to power by legal means. At the same time, he could not reject the cooperation of the revolutionary elements in the Movement, of which the SA was leader. In this way, in August 1930, the

Stennes Revolt developed. By suppressing it, Hitler opened the way the following year to the Harzburg Agreement with the Deutschnationale Volkspartei run by the millionaire Hugenberg, and used the arrangement to seize power legally in 1933.

The previously mentioned Heinrich Bennecke unearthed a significant document at the Institute for Contemporary History in Munich. Its authors were SA departmental heads from the Pomeranian region supporting Stennes. The document concluded with the declaration that 'the NSDAP departed from the course of National Socialist revolution by aligning itself in a reactionary front of a coalition party and in this way abandoned – whether deliberately or not – the old ideals for which we are fighting'.* These were strong words, but many of us would have appended our signatures to this paper and declared openly and fervidly in favour of its contents, as did Horst Wessel in his speech praised by Goebbels. The 'Horst Wessel' hymn, which from 1933 formed part of the German national anthem and was sung an infinite number of times by countless million Germans, has these lines:

> *Kameraden, die Rotfront und Reaktion erschossen,*
> *Marschieren im Geist in unseren Reihen mit*[†]

And now we, Hitler's SA men, were supposed to march, arm in arm with those very people we considered to be the reactionaries? There were many of us who refused to go along with it. A rebel like Stennes fired us up more than those conservatives within the Party devoted to the nobility, such as Göring, Wagener, Frick and many others. In this atmosphere I took my decision to join the SA on 1 May 1931.

Unlike Stennes I never knew Horst Wessel personally. When I joined the SA the hero of our Movement had already been

* IfZ Munich, document Fa88 Fasc.325 sheet 13/15.
† 'Comrades shot dead by the Red Front and Reaction,
  March in spirit with us in our ranks.'

murdered by the 'Red Front', was already one of the dead comrades mentioned in his song. By chance I met his sister Inge, and we got on so well that we worked together for some time on literary matters. We had both graduated from the University of Rostock and met again at the house of a student from the Faculty of Medicine – he had been my best friend at secondary school in Berlin, and we obtained our school-leaving certificates together. Inge and my friend now faced difficult examinations in physics and were busy swotting. Both got excellent grades. Personally I was only interested in Inge Wessel as the sister of the SA man who had not only been the commander of the famed No.5 Company, but a shining example throughout his whole life to his brave death. Inge Wessel did not share my enthusiasm for her brother. Whenever I started talking about him she would pull a face. Naturally, she would not actually make disparaging remarks, for after all he was her brother by blood and had become a person of interest to the public within the political system of the Weimar Republic.

Inge Wessel was no fan of Goebbels, without whose intense propagandizing Horst Wessel would never have basked posthumously in heroic glory. Goebbels got to know her soon after the death of her brother. With an inborn instinct, perhaps by virtue of his physical disability, Goebbels realized at once that he was rejected by the females of the Wessel family. The father, a Protestant pastor with healthy nationalist sentiments, had died some time previously. The younger son, Werner, also an SA man, had lost his life a few weeks before in a skiing accident in the Sudeten mountains. 'The poor woman', Goebbels noted laconically in his diary, 'such a short time after Werner.'* This was on 15 January 1930, a day after the cowardly attack by the Red commune on Horst Wessel, which Goebbels attached great importance to. A few days after he wrote of the mother again: 'A true German woman,' and on

---

* *Die Tagebücher von Joseph Goebbels* (Frölich).

10 February when no hope remained that her son would survive, 'Poor, pitiful woman.' Before 1930 was out he invited mother and daughter to dine at the Hotel Fürstenhof. This was on 23 December 1930, and the same day he noted that they were 'good and pleasant people'.

His positive view of the survivors of the Wessel family suffered a bitter reverse just before the seizure of power in 1933. In memory of Horst Wessel, Goebbels had organized a demonstration both audacious and provocative outside the central office of the KPD (Communist Party), Haus Liebknecht. Apart from Hitler, he had invited the attendance of those closest to the deceased hero. The two central figures, mother and daughter, arrived half an hour late. The atmosphere was charged with nervous tension. The Nazi Party leadership was waiting together with 30,000 SA men including No. 5 Company. Skulking in the surrounding area were gangs of the Communist League of the Red Front, and the police were distributed strategically ready for any eventuality. The two ladies appeared with the nonchalance of royalty and without the least sign of any apology. To top it all, they brought along a retinue including two priests, both of whom held forth. 'Ghastly,' Goebbels confided to his diary on 23 January 1933 – 'whole worlds separate us.' And later: 'Frau Wessel intolerable in her arrogance.' Hitler was as indignant as Goebbels – who described Hitler's speech in the final act as 'short and bad. He must have been very upset.'

In 1936 there was another upset with Frau Wessel at the time of the launching of the naval training brigantine *Horst Wessel*. The mother was to do the honours. Goebbels wrote: 'That crowned it all. She never deserved a son like that.' He was extremely annoyed. The mother had sued in the family court for the rights to the 'Horst Wessel' lyrics. Goebbels stayed the proceedings and wrote about the measures taken on 30 June 1936: 'In the long run we cannot keep it as the national anthem

Adolf Hitler and Ernst Röhm (partially shown at left) at an SA ceremony. Jacob Grimminger holds the 'Bloodied Banner'.

Above: A National Socialist shock troop in Munich. The flag is that of Imperial Germany.

Below left: SA standard bearer with escort. The flag design is one of the first although the photograph was taken in 1930.

Below right: Jacob Grimminger holds the 'Bloodied Banner' alongside Hitler.

Above: Hitler grasps the 'Bloodied Banner' during a National Socialist ceremony.

Below: Ceremony consecrating a new 'Flag of the Old Guard', 15 June 1937. Partially hidden to the left of the flag is Rudolf Hess.

Above: SA members in a march-past at the Brandenburg Gate bearing swastika banners.

Below left: Franz Felix Pfeffer von Salomon (1888–1968) led the SA as Supreme SA-Führer (OSAF) from 1 November 1926 until 29 August 1930.

Below right: Led by the banner of SA Regiment *Horst Wessel*, twelve other standards are paraded before the University of Berlin.

Above: Horst Wessel (standing, extreme right) entered the Nazi Party on 7 December 1926 and became one of its most famous martyrs.

Below left: Adolf Hitler greets an SA member during the 1931 Nuremberg Rally.

Below right: Ernst Röhm (1887–1934) was SA Chief of Staff from 5 January 1931 until his death on 30 June 1934.

Above: SA chief Viktor Lütze delivering a speech at the 1938 Party Congress. Right to left in the audience behind him are Göring, Hess, Streicher, Hitler, Himmler, Ley, Goebbels, Frick and Rosenberg.

Below: A 'family' photo of an SA group in the 1930s.

Above left: SA chief Viktor Lütze.

Above right: Former air ace Hermann Göring as an SA leader in the 1920s.

Below left: An SA parade at Tempelhof airfield, Berlin.

Below right: Hitler at the consecration of the SA 'Red Earth' standard, 1938.

Above: Wilfred von Oven.

Below: Heinrich Himmler during the Beer Hall Putsch of 1923, bearing the banner for Röhm's SA unit, the Reichskriegsflagge, the imperial German ensign.

Above: A Nazi youth rally on 1 May 1933. From left to right: State Secretary Dr Otto Meisner, Vice-Chancellor Franz von Papen, Hitler, Goebbels.

Below: Goebbels in 1933.

... we need a new text ... we cannot scrap it altogether at the moment.'

The graceless attempt by the two women to collect the royalties by litigation were unsuccessful. However, what the mother failed to do the daughter achieved, if in more modest form. She wrote a quite successful book *My Brother Horst – A Legacy* which was in its fifth reprint by 1937. My literary collaboration with her began in 1933 when she published the first volume of a series for scheduled annual releases entitled *The New Book for Girls*. She asked if I would write a story for inclusion following the promises of renowned authors such as Boris von Münchhausen, Heinrich Anacker, Gerhard Schumann, Otto Paust, Martin Luserke and others. I agreed, and a short story of mine appeared in the first volume – for a modest remuneration – located in South America. I never imagined then that I would spend more than forty years of my life in that continent in exile.

I delivered this literary effort under the pseudonym Ewald von Oesterlitz which I registered officially in the Reichsschriftumskammer (Reich Literary Chamber). After the war I illegally used another pseudonym, Willy Oehm, while in a refugee camp in Schleswig-Holstein, and later in Argentina as an occasional correspondent for various West German journals. I soon lost Inge Wessel to sight, but at the time of writing I hear that she is still practising medicine in Bielefeld, the birthplace of her brother Horst.

To return to Horst Wessel and his song. Goebbels was no doubt right with his criticism of it, arguing that it did not harmonize with the immortal melody of the German national anthem 'Das Deutschland Lied' composed by Haydn with a noble text by Hoffmann von Fallersleben. On the other hand it is neither a bad nor ugly song, nor was it plagiarized, as contemporary authors allege now and again. The melody was undoubtedly the work of the musician and lyricist Peter

Cornelius (1824–74) whose principal offering was the comic opera *The Barber of Baghdad*, staged successfully on numerous occasions even in the twentieth century. In a letter written by Cornelius from Munich in 1865, where the Royal School of Music performed, he set down neatly the musical notes which the SA would employ in the distant future. Cornelius's text corresponding to the music appears in the same letter: 'If you love me, I do not fear death'.*

After Cornelius this pleasant melody was used by Horst Wessel. When at age 20 he wrote his own text for SA No. 5 Company, there were already a dozen other texts to fit the melody. The song 'Der Kreuzer *Königsberg*' ('The Cruiser *Königsberg*') must have been what the young SA company commander had in mind when he sat at the piano in his home and sang the song to his family with his own text. His sister used to say: 'At last we have found a song to match the Internationale of the Communists.' On a propaganda tour of Frankfurt/Oder he and his men sang it to the public and reaped fervid approval. Goebbels soon arranged to have it sung at all the unforgettable demonstrations in the Sports Palace, the first time on 7 January 1930. The 'Horst Wessel' became an institution in official National Socialist ceremonial. Its far-sighted words became reality:

Bald flattern Hitler-fahnen über allen Strassen[†]

The owner of the flat which Horst Wessel occupied in the Friedrichshaim district wanted to increase his rent by 3 RM. He was not disposed to accept this, with good reason. The landlord's wife told him that he would see what would happen to him if he did not pay up, and went to see her Red Front neighbours to canvass support. A blackguard, Albrecht 'Ali' Höhler, quickly agreed, and on the afternoon of

---

* Heinz Knobloch, *Der arme Epstein*, Berlin, 1993.
[†] 'Soon Hitler's flags will wave above all streets'.

14 January 1930 teamed up with two thugs to 'teach his SA adversary a lesson', as the Reds used to say. Ali took a loaded pistol along, and the gang proceeded to climb the stairs to Wessel's attic.

Ali had been warned by the landlady that her tenant would be armed, and so before ringing the bell he took out the gun and released the safety catch. When Horst Wessel opened the door Ali shot him in the face without speaking. Wessel collapsed in a pool of blood. His agony lasted six weeks, and on 23 February 1930, wasted away to a bag of bones, he died in the same hospital where he had been first admitted.

During the funeral on 1 March at the Nikolai cemetery, the Bolshevists surrounded the walls and hurled the usual insults, calling the victim 'a blackguard of Hitler' and so forth. The explanation of the whole event was penned in the factory of lies, the Communist Party HQ on Bülow Square, by Willy Münzenberg. The murder, purely political, did not fit into the Red propaganda programme comfortably at that point. The Communists were also aiming to seize power by legal means after the violence they had employed since 1918 had let them down. For this reason Münzenberg invented the story that it had been the simple squaring of accounts between two paid thugs.

The murderer was soon identified and received six years and one months' imprisonment, a surprisingly long sentence for a person defended by the cunning and corrupt Communist Party member Hilda Benjamin.* After the war she rose to be Vice-President of the DDR Supreme Court where she dished out justice under her nickname 'the Red Guillotine'. The DDR government maintained Münzenberg's version of the event until

---

* It amounted to a sentence of death. Höhler was still serving his sentence when Hitler came to power in 1933. That same year, while being moved from one prison to another, Höhler was abducted by SA men and shot. His accomplices keeping lookout at the Horst Wessel murder, Epstein and Zieger, were re-tried and executed.

its dissolution in 1989. The Western democratic re-education system also accepts it to the present day. After 1945 the graves of Horst Wessel and his father were desecrated and then destroyed by the liberators.

CHAPTER 10

Democratic Checks and Balances to Control Adolf Hitler

The young student and SA company commander, who in his song had his murdered comrades marching in spirit in the SA ranks, did not come from the working class, and even less from amongst the criminals and blackguards of his killer. That year, Gauleiter Goebbels wrote an article with the simple title 'Horst' for his 'spoiled child' the journal *Der Angriff*. This was initially a monthly publication, but from 1 October 1929 a weekly and finally, from 1 November 1930, a daily, subtitled *The German Evening Newspaper of Berlin*.* In his article Goebbels referred to Horst Wessel, 'Our Horst' as we his comrades and also his own Gauleiter used to call him. In simple words, 'without pathos nor hackneyed phrases' as he expressed it, he sketched through that figure 'the face of the Germany of tomorrow … for which it is worth the struggle of living'.†

To live and to die, as 200 SA men would do who fell for a better Reich – young men such as ourselves were examples worthy of honour and it was for that reason that we enlisted in the SA and marched together towards that 'brilliant dawn' announced by Goebbels. One place where we did not march was the town of Harzburg, where on 11 October 1931 the alliance convened to form the 'National Opposition'. Hitler would not have been keen on our presence in this idyllic spa

---

* Joseph Goebbels, *Wetterleuchten. Aufsätze aus der Kampfzeit*, Munich, 1939, quote from 9 October 1930.
† Ibid.

town, situated on the northern slopes of the Harz mountains. We would not have prevented the pact with the Deutsch-Nationale Partei, but we could have caused many unpleasant problems. Hitler could not reveal to us his true intentions so as not to destroy the illusions of those who believed they could use him to seize power themselves and then deal him the coup-de-grace. Papen admitted as much after the war (1952) with a wealth of details and self-importance in his book *A Break with the Truth*. Professor Robert Wistrich of the Hebrew University of Jerusalem pointed to Papen's 'infinite self-esteem', a matter upon which, to tell the truth, one cannot contradict him.*

The Harzburger Front, the tactical pact between the NSDAP and the German Nationalists plus Stahlhelm, was signed without consulting the SA, which was not even represented. Goebbels stripped the pact of any importance in an article published in his *Der Angriff* on 21 October 1931, calling the agreement 'a mere formality'. The NSDAP had its own programme and was not proposing to amend it. Its current purpose was to achieve the intermediate goal of engineering the fall of the incompetent government of Dr Heinrich Brüning, who as a trade unionist and politician of the Centre was on the point of governing exclusively by emergency decree, applying a mistaken political economy and an agenda of prohibitions leading directly to misery and later chaos.

The situation arrived just six months later. In mid-1932 unemployment reached six million, and soon passed it. On 13 April 1932, the 300,000-strong SA was banned under Article 48 of the Emergencies Act. When another of Brüning's emergency decrees managed to offend the agricultural sector, already in dire straits because of the general economic policy, he made himself an enemy of President Hindenburg, who had interests in farming. On 30 May Hindenburg asked for his resignation, which was presented immediately and accepted with equal

* Robert Wistrich, *Who's Who in Nazi Germany*, London, 1982.

speed. This achieved the intermediate goal. The Harzburg Front should now have collapsed, but was seen as indispensable for the ultimate objective. Goebbels put it mildly by forecasting that 'the seizure of power can now only be achieved by a coalition'.

The young men of the SA heard the message but like Faust lacked faith. For us, the German Nationalists and their armed branch, the Stahlhelm, continued to be the reactionaries to whom Horst Wessel referred in his song. Our vision of the future was very different to theirs. We wanted a revolutionary future, ultimately a National Socialist future, a fresh start for Germany. Out of this the unease, one might say the spirit of rebellion, which had calmed since the Stennes crisis in 1930, revived, and the fact that it had did not escape the political instincts of Goebbels.

The thinking behind his article in *Der Angriff* was to head us off, and he put the idea to Hitler that immediately after Harzburg, an SA demonstration should be organized at Brunswick, a town which had become an SA fortress. We did not want to go to Harzburg, but did not mind marching through Brunswick. More than 100,000 arrived at the home town of Henry the Lion, Duke of Bavaria and Saxony (1129–95). The march was a great success.

'Harzburg was an intermediate stage', Goebbels wrote in *Der Angriff* on 27 October 1931, 'but Brunswick was the proclamation of the ultimate goal.' The person who indicated this ultimate goal with emphatic clarity was Adolf Hitler. At Harzburg they tried to push him aside as a minority partner within a national alliance. This had also been Kahr's intention in 1923: leave him to beat the drum while the reactionary big-wigs held on to the reins of power. For that reason they had been allowed to open fire on the National Socialists at the Feldherrnhalle in Munich.

After their release from Landsberg, Hitler and his followers had had to seek a new beginning. They had succeeded and could now, eight years later, hammer with growing insistence on the doors of power. 'We awoke Germany,' Goebbels wrote, and rightly. We believed we had carried our grain of sand, not only by spreading the slogan *'Deutschland erwache!'*, but by our physical intervention. In *Der Angriff* Goebbels continued to emphasize that Adolf Hitler was 'not only the inspired drummer who awakens the Germans but also the intelligent tactician and visionary statesman appointed by destiny to pull this country back from the abyss'. The brand of policies practised since 1918 was at its last gasp, Goebbels maintained: 'At Harzburg the opposition front combined; at Brunswick the army of the political offensive marched.'

Our adversaries knew this. The 'Sozis' – our name for the Social Democrats – tried to stop us after Harzburg with what they called 'The Iron Front', composed of the Reichsbanner of Röhm's crony Hauptmann Mayr and some trade unions, but it was soon clear that the Iron Front was not up to the job. We were proud of the successes achieved by Hitler's Movement and did not play down our support for it. Stennes had apparently over-rated the Iron Front to the extent that he had had to give ground to Hitler and admit that the SA was an important factor within the NSDAP. As we knew, Hitler would always ask: 'What would the SA say about this' every time he had to make a decision of importance. He knew that our opinion on Harzburg was negative. Therefore he consulted with Goebbels on the best way to put across the idea of a coalition, bearing in mind our opposition to it. The result was the previously mentioned editorial to which Goebbels gave the title 'From Harzburg to Brunswick'.

The affair rumbled on. I can still recall clearly how it was debated in our company. It was not at all certain that it would be accepted just because it came down 'from above'. Certainly we shared the principles of order and discipline as being necessary within a military-type organization, but we were not zombies. We had our own opinions and wanted to defend them, or at least be persuaded by better argument just as the ancient Germanic peoples had been allowed in their assemblies. Here the king or prince was required to accede to the resolutions approved by the majority. In fact, we felt the need for something similar, a democratic system of checks and balances for the leadership elected by us.

The Nazi leadership did not want us to have such a control mechanism. Accordingly I drew my own conclusions and on 1 May 1932 resigned from both the SA and the Party. My section commander was astonished when I told him. After recovering from the shock he asked me: 'Oven, we are a step away from taking power and you want to resign?' I replied that as I saw it, there were enough men available to enable the Movement to become the government. I was dispensable. Contrary to what he and I both expected, I never suffered any inconvenience for resigning. Nobody cared. I was now free to dedicate my time to starting my profession as a writer instead of having to share it with the NSDAP and the SA (at that time banned!).

I had taken a close look into the possible consequences of resigning from both bodies beforehand, and what I discovered corresponded with the regulations included much later in the NSDAP Book of Enrolments: 'Service in the SA is and will remain voluntary. Just as the invitation to join promises no advantage or boon, neither does it exercise any force upon anybody to join. The SA man is at liberty to resign if he finds himself not in agreement with the political line of the institution. The SA man can resign with honour if his motives are honourable.'* I had my motives. I was given an honourable discharge which was registered in the Party's central card-index system.

I remained in friendly contact with Stennes and his rebellious ideas through my Berlin-Wedding comrade whom I mentioned

* *Organisationsbuch der NSDAP*, Munich, 1936.

earlier, although during the final year of the struggle before 1933 and the first years afterwards we lost sight of each other. We were both earning our living as journalists. We were soon back in uniform, not brown but field-grey. Günter did not turn his back on the Party as I did, but with good political instinct exchanged the SA for the SS. From there he had no problem in advancing into the National Socialist Press corps. As a 'renegade' I had to take courses at the School for Journalists, Berlin-Dahlem, in order to register as a professional. I passed the examinations 'with distinction'.

The first organ to hire me was none other than *Der Angriff*. After a few months I went to Hugenberg's Scherl house, which paid me better. There I worked in the news section. In 1938 the firm sent me to Spain as the first German journalist to follow the Condor Legion during the Spanish Civil War. I returned to Berlin with the Legion in May 1939 to be met by my wife and son. My economic situation had improved greatly: I had a car and bank account! In August 1939 I was called up and drafted to an Army propaganda company. It was there that I ran into Stennes again.

Our former SA commander had been out of the picture for some time. His eternal carping and grumbling during the early 1930s had so irked them that in the end they offered him a job at the military mission in China. This was in 1933. He had married in 1930, Hitler sending him a somewhat frosty telegram of congratulations. The other important leadership guest invited who turned up was Goebbels. 'He was my most likeable guest,' the young bride confessed to the British author and spy Drage, 'far and away the most intelligent, had the best manners, was attentive and a delightful conversationalist.'* In his diary entry for 18 December 1930 Goebbels makes no mention of the bride at this wedding although he was pleased by the male participants and even the groom, who had caused

---

* Drage, *Als Hitler nach Canossa ging*.

him so many upsets and headaches. 'They are great lads,' he wrote in his diary in Berlin ink. 'All were very attentive to me – most of all Stennes.' And later: 'One has to know how to treat them. Evidently Munich did not.'* 'Berlin' – Goebbels – had a better understanding than 'Munich' (Hitler) for the problems of the Berliners, as for all the SA companies north of the Kraut Line (an imaginary line formed by the River Meno separating the South – Bavaria – from the North – Prussia, these being the eternal antagonists.

I have written briefly about the problem of the 'democratic checks and balances' idea within an authoritarian movement – as I saw the Berlin SA – not only because it was my reason for resigning from the NSDAP and the SA, but also because it speaks volumes for a Propaganda Minister who would have this 'renegade' in his intimate home environment for two whole years. For me, Goebbels was the shining example of Germanic loyalty. His physical deformity did not coincide with the racial ideals of our epoch. His loyalty is reflected nowadays in Hollywood productions: the man who accepted death for himself and his entire family rather than that they should be exposed to the opprobrium of an enemy consumed with hate. Stennes, whom I consider the revolutionary prototype, and Goebbels both shared my own ideas regarding democracy – not that which emerged from the pernicious birth of the French Revolution, that is to say the liberal form – but one which accepts the idea of the corrective mechanism which prevailed in Germanic antiquity.

Nazism had to have such a mechanism. Goebbels underlines its importance and necessity repeatedly. Stennes was not opposed to it, but moved within a much more modest political perspective. His squabbles with Munich were not so much about the matters mentioned in this chapter, but rather about money and influence for the SA. When both were refused, he

* *Die Tagebücher von Joseph Goebbels* (Frölich).

rebelled. When forced to submit to Hitler he resigned, married and later accepted the post of military adviser to Jiang Jieshi at Nanjing.

He only got there once the Gestapo had finished with him. His escape was no easy matter. He was arrested for the first time in March 1933, and on occasions thereafter. Curiously he was never detained long. 'Without any doubt, Göring saved my life,' he told his British friend Drage, for nothing else seemed to explain it. Possibly it had to do with their mutual past in a corps of cadets. Certainly Göring would have helped – previously he had been the superior of Gestapo organizer Rudolf Diels as head of the Prussian government and was interested in Stennes's welfare. As Prussian Interior Minister, Göring had ordered Diels, who had immediate responsibility for the prisoner, to transfer him to Columbia Haus in Berlin and to keep an eye on him personally, but the main support for the old SA chief – the 'fox in the henhouse' who had contributed so much to the National Socialist rise to power – came from an unexpected corner – the Catholic Church.

Walther Stennes had the good fortune to be the nephew of Cardinal Karl Joseph Schulte (1871–1941), Archbishop of Cologne. As one of the highest ecclesiastical dignitaries of Germany, the Archbishop had access to the Führer without intermediaries. He knew positively that Hitler would not deny his request to set his nephew at liberty, particularly when his petition was supported by the Papal nuncio, Cesare Orsenigo – with whom Hitler had worked out the Concordat with the Vatican on 20 July 1933. Hitler agreed, on the condition that Stennes left the country discreetly and at once. This coincided with Stennes's intentions. On 26 August 1933 he was freed by the Gestapo and next day, after taking leave of his parents, crossed the border into Holland. From there he reached England and was reunited with his wife. Together they embarked for the Far East, where he took up his new post.

It is an astonishing fact that this political adventurer was able to slip away in the daily bustle of Hitler's Germany by reason of an event at the outset of the Third Reich which aided Hitler to govern as dictator for twelve years: the Concordat with the Catholic Church, the first state treaty signed by Hitler as head of state. With it he was able to establish the legal conditions for a fruitful relationship between the German Reich and the Church of Rome. From then on there was a Papal nuncio in Berlin and a German ambassador at the Vatican, sent by a Nazi Germany even today denigrated as 'atheist'. Hitler was excommunicated by the Church later for being the best man at Goebbels's marriage to his wife Magda, a divorcée, and remained excommunicated until he entered Valhalla at his death; he refused to pay his personal ecclesiastic tax as an excommunicatee.

In Berlin the Vatican was represented by the nuncio. The bishops were required to swear an oath of loyalty to the state before taking office, promising to include in their Sunday sermons mentions of the Reich and its Führer. In return, the Reich agreed to establish and collect the ecclesiastical tax on behalf of the Church. The consent of the local Gauleiter was increasingly important from then on in the appointment of bishops. These and other agreements between the parties promised a beneficial and lasting collaboration between government and Church. The ex-SA chief and rebel Walther Stennes was one of the first to benefit from this Concordat thanks to his uncle, the Archbishop and Cardinal of Cologne and the Papal nuncio in Germany, Cesare Orsenigo.

Sixteen years later, in June 1949, Stennes returned home to the Federal Republic of West Germany, a structure erected by the victorious Western powers. As with every West German citizen, he and I had to submit to the process of 'denazification'. He was classified Group V, 'Not Involved' and exempted from all restrictions and penalties. Once the new money, the

Deutschmark, was introduced at the beginning of the 'German economic miracle', Stennes had the cheek to sue the new government for 'damages' and 'loss of earnings' suffered during the period of the National Socialist 'terrorist' regime, in which he was, so he alleged, 'a victim of persecution'. His claim was thrown out, and he was no more successful in his attempts to enter politics. He died a very old man, totally forgotten by the public.

CHAPTER 11

Worms and Other Political Reptiles

Of the fourteen Chancellors who steered the Weimar Republic during its fourteen-year existence, General Kurt von Schleicher (1882–1934) was the last. His term of office was also the shortest, scarcely two months, from 3 December 1932 to 28 January 1933.

Schleicher spent the First World War as a young General Staff officer with the Army Railway Administration-General. During the first confused immediate postwar years he was in the General Staff of Hans von Seeckt, appointed Army Commander-in-Chief after the Kapp putsch of March 1920. Seeckt is given great credit for creating the standing army of 100,000 men which the victors allowed Germany by the Treaty of Versailles. It was to Seeckt, appointed a general by the Kaiser, that Schleicher undoubtedly owed the realization of most of his political ambitions which, in the end, would result in his death by shooting on 30 June 1934.

When Seeckt retired in 1926, Schleicher made politics his chosen profession. He entered the Reichstag as a Nationalist deputy and also began writing. When the advent of the Third Reich threatened, he abandoned both activities to concentrate on opposing National Socialism and Hitler. He intrigued against Hitler with members of the NSDAP hierarchy such as Gregor Strasser. His lust for power and contempt for adversity, qualities linked to treacherous cunning, put him amongst other dubious personalities working furtively for the 'nationalist opposition'. Schleicher in German is the noun describing a person who 'worms his way into somebody's confidence' and rarely was a person so aptly named as per Plautus' dictum *nomen est omen*.

His brief but glittering performance on the stage of German Weimar history began when General Wilhelm Groener (1867–1939), former chief of the Army Railway Administration-General, summoned him in 1929 to occupy the principal post in a section created for him in the Reichswehr Ministry. Probably very few knew what this office did. During the 1918 revolution, Groener had had charge of the logistics department left vacant by Ludendorff, and as such was one of the principal actors responsible for the abdication of Kaiser Wilhelm II when he informed His Majesty that he could no longer count on the loyalty of his troops. Groener first made contact after the war with Friedrich Ebert of the SPD (Social Democratic Party), the honest and sincere belt-maker who, from November 1918, headed the 'Council of Deputies of the People' and planned the course of German politics. Ebert rewarded Groener for his support by appointing him – since he was an ex-railway general – Minister of Transport, an office which he exchanged for the War Ministry in 1928. From that point onwards his right-hand man was General von Schleicher.

Schleicher was very important to Groener for having begun his military career with the 3rd Foot Guards Regiment where his commanding officer had been Paul von Hindenburg, now Reich President, following the death of Ebert in February 1925. Groener had helped get Ebert elected President and could count on a reliable ally in the new Chancellor, Kurt von Schleicher. The Hindenburg–Groener–Schleicher triumvirate of generals was based exclusively in the apolitical Reichswehr during this sad and desolate epoch of social and economic oppression. The economy was crumbling, unemployment soaring and one weak government gave way to another equally weak. In this situation, on 14 September 1930, the NSDAP stood in the elections for the fifth legislative period since the war.

As has been described, these elections resulted in a true political landslide when 107 NSDAP deputies returned, the second largest grouping after the Social Democrats, whose share of the seats had fallen to 143. Political circles were now alarmed to notice that Hitler was at the gates! There was still a long way to go of course. As in 1918, the Groener–Schleicher duo believed it was time to act and they concentrated their attentions and efforts on SA Chief of Staff Ernst Röhm, whom Hitler had summoned from Bolivia to transform the SA into the political arm to guarantee that the NSDAP would take power.

For Britain and France, Groener was an acceptable negotiator. He had shown his aptitude as a politician submissive to these foreign interests by his decisive intervention to ensure the collapse of the Second Reich and the launch of the Republican system. London and Paris lived in hope that the grave-digger of the Second Reich could prevent the birth of the Third. For this reason they thought they might loosen a little bit the bonds which had kept the Reich restrained since the Treaty of Versailles was signed, and give Groener a little more backbone to stand up to 'the brown battalions'.

For knowledge of this important historical detail we are indebted to former SA general and later Gauleiter of Magdeburg province, Rudolf Jordan (1902–1984) Coming from a lower middle-class family, at a tender age he joined the juvenile Catholic Movement which lent support to the armaments industry during the First World War. In 1920 he volunteered for the Reichswehr, then after qualifying as a primary school teacher set out to become a politician. He spoke on the hustings everywhere, but never adhered to any particular party. Shortly after the re-foundation of the NSDAP in 1925, on 15 May that year he became member 4,871. Moving up the ladder, by 1929 he sat as a magistrate at Fulda and entered the Hesse-Nassau provincial parliament as a deputy. In 1931 he was appointed Gauleiter of Halle-Merseburg, and after 1933, state adviser in Prussia, was elected to the Reichstag and received a series of honorary offices, amongst them appointment as an SA general.*

Throughout his life Jordan felt an intense obligation to serve his country. Thus he weathered the tragic events of 30 June 1934, the final struggle on the Elbe in April and May 1945, and the forty years of horror and disillusion which followed. With his wife and three children he escaped the Soviets by swimming the Elbe, only to be captured by the British, passed to the Americans and then handed over to the Soviets. After passing through various prisons and concentration camps he finished up in the Lubianka for trial and received twenty-five years' forced labour. In 1951 a German court declared him dead, but this was only half-true. Despite the tortures, Soviet labour camps and malnutrition, on 13 October 1955, following the intevention of Chancellor Konrad Adenauer, the emaciated idealist was repatriated with the majority of German PoWs who would ever get home. He used the years preceding his death in Munich in 1984 to correct and give shape to many historical details of importance, including those relating to the SA.

In his dalliance with the British and French in the pre-Hitler period, Schleicher warned them that the results of the September 1930 elections provided Hitler with a springboard to power. Schleicher was taking advantage of his good relationship with the British Foreign Office and French Minister Edouard Daladier (1884–1970), which Groener had been able to cement during the time when he occupied the offices of Reichswehr Minister and Foreign Minister. Apparently London was not worried about a Reichswehr strengthened in quality and numbers, provided it remained in the hands of trustworthy friends such as Brüning, Groener and Schleicher; quite the contrary: they were even giving the nod to those compliant

* Karl Höffkes, *Hitlers politische Generale*, Tübingen, 1986,
    pp. 159–64.

German politicians who were saying that a strong Reichswehr would be the best guarantee to keep Hitler out.

This was one of the roots of the incomprehensible and unnatural antagonism between the Reichswehr and the SA. I, and certainly all my comrades, always thought of the Reichswehr as a friendly institution and potential ally in our fight against the Marxist-dominated Republican regime. As a boy in the Silesian town of Liegnitz, where my grandfather, the retired commander of a cavalry squadron, had settled, I knew the local Reichswehr well because officers would often drop by to ask my grandfather's advice. Later, a musician from the Reichswehr military band gave me instruction in the flute. Neither in Liegnitz, nor afterwards in Berlin, did anybody think that the national armed force was a competitor, even less an enemy.

Ernst Röhm was therefore the man chosen to turn the SA into the strong and flexible instrument which National Socialism needed to gain power. On 5 January 1931 he took over his new command. His title was 'Supreme SA and SS Führer'. Supreme *command* over both organizations was a different thing and remained in the hands of Hitler. Röhm committed himself to absolute obedience. His first measures were organizational. He eliminated errors, instructed his subordinate officers in military procedures and increased the membership to numbers undreamt of. From 77,000 SA men registered in January 1931, the number rose rapidly to 100,000 and later that year to 260,438. This incredible increase was not exclusively Röhm's doing, however. The disastrous economic policies of the Brüning government of the centre-left and the excessive use of the decree-cudgel by the executive organs ensured that the unemployed youth of Germany flowed in massive numbers into the SA. One year after Röhm assumed power over the SA, it outnumbered the Reichswehr by two to one.

These disproportionate numbers provided Schleicher, at that moment the most important man in the Reichswehr Ministry and from May 1932 its head, with ammunition for his secret negotiations with London and Paris. The British and French wanted him to enlarge the Reichswehr to a size capable of easily opposing Röhm's growing SA. These aims could not be realized because the regime was too weak and Schleicher's intrigues left him a man not to be completely trusted. The growing Reichswehr–SA controversy which had been sparked off on 11 October 1931 at Bad Harzburg for the purpose of creating the so-called 'Nationalist Opposition' was becoming ever more acute. To take power, Hitler needed not only the numerically strong SA, which Röhm was organizing with visible success, but also a great deal of money and the patronage of industrial and banking circles. Hugenberg and his Deutsch-Nationale Volkspartei (DNVP) was one of those circles. In the recent election the DNVP had lost almost half its seats and therefore needed urgently a manageable partner with which to form a coalition. This partner could be the NSDAP, which had grown so spectacularly, but its leader would have to undertake to respect the Reichswehr, support Harzburg and all conservative forces. For this reason, the SA could not be involved in the events at Harzburg, although a week later they allowed us to march in Brunswick, where the NSDAP held a major position in the provincial government. There was no ban on wearing uniforms at Brunswick as there was in Berlin. We wanted – and were required – to provide a show of force, and that we did very successfully.

During October and November 1931, the eternal merchant of intrigue Schleicher had his first meeting with Hitler, organized by Röhm. We know this from Jordan's notes. For Hitler the meeting looked interesting because of Schleicher's contacts to his regimental comrade, Reich President Paul von Hindenburg and his son Oskar. The Weimar constitution gave the President very wide powers. Even with a majority of seats in the Reichstag, the winning party did not necessarily take power automatically, if the President did not favour it. Schleicher, obviously, had no intention of aiding Hitler, and did not intrigue for the sake of it, but as a way to 'open his umbrella' at a judicious time for the eventuality that Hitler might win and become Chancellor. Jordan revealed that on 29 January 1933, that is, the day before Hindenburg appointed Hitler Reich Chancellor, Schleicher proposed that Hitler should make him Reichswehr Minister. The sitting Minister, General von Hammerstein-Equord (later associated with the Resistance, and who suggested having Hitler imprisoned in 1939) made the same proposal. Jordan recorded without comment that both proposals were rejected,

1932 was, for the SA, perhaps the most difficult in its existence. One election followed another at all political levels. None could be won without the active presence of the SA. In a huge National Socialist rally at Nuremberg, Hitler told the SA: 'What you are, you are thanks to me: and what I am, I am thanks to you.' This was both a confession and a promise. We were proud of what he had said, and as a result went to work with a will. We were in action day after day, sometimes night after night.

In March 1932, Hitler offered himself as a candidate for Reich President, and obtained 11.34 million votes. Hindenburg failed to obtain the 50 per cent necessary to win the nomination outright despite Social Democrat support, but succeeded in the second round on 10 April. The NSDAP increased its share again, and this was the motive for the emergency decree banning the SA presented to the Reichstag by Groener three days after the presidential election.

The ban on the SA was not very damaging for the NSDAP. The enormous corps of young activists now 'without work' was used by the Party to clear the administrative backlog. All of us then, without exception, were Nazi Party members (today of course they all deny it) and were therefore available to work in the offices. Personally, this kind of office-boy (or 'lapdog' as we termed it) activity seemed purposeless to us, although it did not annoy me anything like as much as the repeated meetings in smoke-filled bars where old men with large stomachs held heated discussions on matters which to us seemed irrelevant.

The ban on the SA by decree was without doubt undemocratic. The swelling numbers experienced by the Movement nationwide in parallel with the endless stream of provincial elections possibly influenced Chancellor Brüning to throw in his hand. Hindenburg accepted the resignation at once and appointed Franz von Papen in his place at Schleicher's suggestion. Like Brüning, Papen was a member of the Catholic Centre Party. The Party was not keen on the appointment but neither Hindenburg nor Papen cared, and in any case the new Chancellor solved the problem simply by resigning from the Party. For this he had to pay the price of losing the Party whip, which left him adrift at the mercy of the President and his emergency decrees. Papen's Cabinet was dubbed 'The Cabinet of the Barons'. (A part of it entered Hitler's Cabinet on 30 January 1933 when Papen became Vice-Chancellor.) In the Reichstag Papen was isolated and could count only on the conservative Right and Hitler's goodwill, which he bought by promising to get the ban on the SA lifted. He kept his word a fortnight later and at the same time cancelled the ban on wearing uniforms.

I did not participate in the election of 31 June 1932 because I was not yet twenty. The results changed the split of seats in the Reichstag completely. The NSDAP was the true victor. At a stroke it had doubled its number of seats from 107 to 230, which made it the strongest grouping, relegating the Social Democrats to second place with 133. Before President Hindenburg could decide whether the leader of this majority party should be the new Chancellor, the suffering populace had to hold out through two more governments after the catastrophic Brüning administration: first Papen and then Schleicher. Neither had political nor popular support. It was the golden era for intriguers and con-men. Its outstanding figure in this respect was Schleicher, who dismissed from office the man he had practically made Chancellor a little before, Papen.

Meanwhile the NSDAP, with a potential of 13.7 million votes, had a million party members and an SA army far exceeding the Reichswehr in size, and was the leader on the political scene. Never had there been a political party so strong and vibrant in the history of the Weimar Republic. The situation demanded a rapid and radical solution. Eventually there happened what had to happen, and on 13 August 1932 President von Hindenburg received Adolf Hitler for the first time. The head of state offered the successful politician the Vice-Chancellorship, a post which Hitler rejected firmly but politely, and again when the offer was repeated a few days later.

The Reichstag was dissolved again. Fresh elections were called. On 6 November 1932 the voters responded with apathy, even the NSDAP supporters. As a result the Party lost thirty-three seats while the Communists gained eleven and now had one hundred. The political panorama was acquiring a critical outline. Schleicher was on the watch for any opportunity. Although a convinced opponent of the Nazis he maintained close contacts with men in Hitler's entourage such as Gregor Strasser, whom many National Socialists considered the most important ideologist of the Movement. Strasser had been the predecessor of Goebbels as head of propaganda and of Robert Ley when head of the Party's general organization. Schleicher now offered Strasser the Vice-Chancellorship in his future Cabinet and the Prime Minister's spot in Prussia. The purpose of this offer was to keep Hitler out of power, but Strasser turned it all down when Hitler objected, and also resigned all his offices within the Movement. Schleicher had to form a new government in December 1932 without the participation of the NSDAP and without a majority in the Reichstag.

After fifty-six days he resigned as Chancellor and was succeeded by Adolf Hitler on 30 January 1933. The population of Berlin celebrated that night with an interminable torchlight parade led by the SA, crossing through the Brandenburg Gate and passing before the Reich Chancellery.

CHAPTER 12

Hitler's Seizure of Power

I did not march with the SA columns which – in all Germany – hailed the 'seizure of power', the realization of a dream celebrated with unparalleled enthusiasm. The bitter drops in the brown battalions' 'cup that runneth over' were the two fatalities that night: Sturmführer Hans Eberhard Maikowski and Police Sergeant Zauritz, both members of No. 33 Company who fell under a rain of bullets when attacked by an armed Communist gang while returning to barracks. We learned of this and many other occurrences from radio broadcasts that historic night.

Amongst the medley of voices the only one I recognized was Gauleiter Joseph Goebbels. I had heard it many times during Party demonstrations in recent years. Within a few weeks from 13 March 1933 onwards, it would become the unmistakable voice of the Reich Propaganda Minister, whose mastery of the spoken word would help build Hitler's empire. The radio reporter was in the midst of a crowd when he found Goebbels and asked him for a quote. His sole comment was 'This is the triumph of tenacity.' Henceforth this phrase would be the motto of his work. The triumph of 30 January 1933 would not be repeated in the war imposed on us in 1939, however,* that was our misfortune to come, and perhaps I knew it as well as any for having spent the last two years of it at Goebbels's side.

On 30 January 1933 I was working as a secretary to another 'man of the pen' although one of lesser importance. He was a fairly leftist intellectual for whom I handled correspondence and

* David Hoggan, *Der erzwungene Krieg*, Tübingen, 1961.

corrected manuscripts. Also to my great joy he had me chauffeur his Buick cabriolet. I enjoyed the work despite the poor pay and its casual nature. That night I was seated near the radio as if entranced. During a pause when I turned to assist my employer I saw that he was packing a suitcase. 'You're taking a trip?' I enquired in surprise. 'This very night,' he replied, 'As far away as I can get. You will drive me to the railway station.' I did so and never saw him again. I did not enquire into the reason for his haste. We always talked and argued a lot, mainly about Hölderlin, Stefan Georg and other poets we both admired, but never about politics. 'I have a bad feeling,' was the only clue he ever gave me to explain his wild flight. I heard he survived the war in Palma de Mallorca while I was in a refugee camp in Schleswig-Holstein.

This fugitive and so many others fitted outside that mass of people to whom Adolf Hitler made his first radio broadcast as Chancellor on 1 February 1933, beginning with a phrase typical of his manner: 'The inheritance we have received is appalling. The confidence we have knows no limits because we believe in the people and their immutable values.'*

My employer apparently did not have that confidence or conviction. For that reason he bolted without giving rhyme nor reason, leaving behind his debts, including what he owed me. He had not expected Hitler's proclamation, missed hearing him say that 'Christianity has to be the basis of our moral duty'. Neither did he hear Hitler promise absolute obedience to President Hindenburg, or his closing prayer: 'May the Almighty take our work into his hands, guide wisely our aims, bless our minds and make us content in the confidence of our people, for we struggle not for ourselves, but for Germany.'

My mother, a very devout Christian evangelical, to whom her National Socialist sons brought many heartaches during the years of struggle, allowed herself to be convinced of the

---

* Max Domarus, *Hitler Reden, 1932–1945*, Wiesbaden, 1973.

goodwill of the new government by these proclamations. The assiduous Archive Director Dr Max Domarus (b. 1922) who recorded these words of Hitler in his voluminous four tomes, does not shy from making harsh criticism of the Führer but admits that the majority of the populace, which until that moment had conceived of Hitler as 'an uncouth carpenter and proletarian agitator' was 'visibly impressed' by the statements.

Even I, who the year before had allowed myself to be stirred up by Stennes and others against Hitler and the Nazi Party, was not only profoundly impressed, but newly and sincerely enthusiastic. Now it distressed me to have turned my back on the Movement, not for any future advantage I might have lost – these things did not count. Now all that mattered was the German people and the political Movement which the leadership had taken into its hands.

In accordance with Hitler's call, I decided to rejoin the ranks I had abandoned nine months before. Thus, a few weeks afterwards, I found myself once more in the office of our SA company in Berlin-Lichterade where in 1931 I had made my initial application to enter its ranks, My intention was now to repeat it.

My former chief, Riewe, was no longer there. No doubt he had been found a new occupation to reward his efforts during the years of struggle. The only man I thought I recognized, in his new brown uniform straight from the factory, was the husband of the lady who ran the greengrocer's on our street corner. When I was last in the SA he had been a player in the band of the Combat League of the Red Front and had fought on the streets against us in battles which resulted in a number of dents and bumps both to himself and his instrument. He recognized me and raised his right hand in the Hitler salute, remembering not to clench his fist as had been his habit in the past. I knew that fist from the number of times it had sped towards my nose at the velocity laid down in the Marxist rule book. I did not return his salute. Possibly this ex-Communist was one of those sincere proletarians who had seen the error of his ways and turned to us, and maybe he would become one of the millions who paid tribute to the Fatherland with their blood during the war to come. Without a word I turned on my heel and returned home more pensive than when I had arrived. My next contact with the NSDAP lay ten years ahead through the Gauleiter of Berlin, who plucked me from the midst of the war reporters corps to serve as his press adjutant. By then the Party was no longer open to me.

The unexpected appearance of the former Red Front musician in the ranks of my old SA company was just one of the many examples of the avalanche of people flooding into the SA. Longerich estimated the membership at 30 January 1933 as 'quite a few less than 500,000 men', and SA General Heinrich Bennecke put it at 300,000.[*] By mid-1934 the total was not 'almost 4.5 million' as Longerich asserts, but was exactly 3,543,009 on 1 January 1935 according to the official NSDAP statistics, also quoted by Bennecke. This figure has to be reduced by the 'Reserve SA I and II' which had been incorporated on 6 November 1933 into the active SA as an automatic measure rather than by individuals volunteering. There were 497,610 Stahlhelm members and 1,376,771 Kyffhäuserbund men and other traditionalist groups and reservists. If we subtract these contingents having an average age of 45 and which inflate the official number as at 1 January 1935, we find that there were fewer than two million SA volunteers direct from the public and not the 'four or five million' which modern historians like to conjure with.[†]

---

[*] Bennecke, *Reichswehr*.

[†] This deception is linked by historians to another lie: the assertion that SA members were all Party members. That was the case until 1933. After then no new members were admitted to the Party, but recruitment to the SA continued. Accordingly, after Hitler seized power, the majority of the two million SA men were not Nazi Party members.

Equally, two million well-trained men within an authoritarian and disciplined political system were a power base like no other in Germany at that time. The counterweight within this Centre–Right coalition installed by President Hindenburg as the government and strictly respecting all the democratic Weimar Republic rules of play, was the 100,000-man standing army of the Reichswehr allowed to Germany by the Treaty of Versailles. (The limitations imposed in respect of the numbers of men and armaments had actually been breached some time previously. It was a fact known to all, not only Berlin, but also London, Washington and Paris. The Kremlin was also aware of the breaches, and like London and Paris had been a party to them.)

A 100,000-man Army was one thing, but two million SA paramilitaries was a serious problem from the point of view of the various foreign governments and the German coalition. The solution was the 'Harzburg Front'. If Papen and the ministers he proposed did not want to lose their influence as a majority in the Reichstag – remembering that of the ten Hitler-Cabinet ministers only Hitler and two others were NSDAP members, Göring and Frick – then it was essential to have a totally reliable man leading the Reichswehr. The man chosen was career officer Werner von Blomberg (1876-1946, died in US internment, even though since 1936 he had lived for ten years in retirement in Bavaria with no further interest in politics). He was the son of a Pomeranian military family. On 30 January 1933 Hindenburg named him Reichswehr Minister in the rank of Generalleutnant, demonstrating the esteem which he had for Blomberg despite the enmity between him and Schleicher. Hindenburg and Blomberg were both from the Prussian aristocracy east of the Elbe: both were robust and of good appearance, and had had significant experience at the front. Both enjoyed much respect even from circles with which they were not in harmony. A generation separated their ages. Hindenburg, a pensioner when the Great War broke out, was recalled to active duty the first day. Scarcely three weeks later he was victor over the Russians at the famous Battle of Tannenberg in East Prussia (August 1914). At this time, Blomberg had barely made lieutenant.

In the official Cabinet list, Blomberg figured in fifth place after Chancellor Hitler, Vice-Chancellor von Papen, Foreign Minister Konstantin von Neurath and Interior Minister Dr Wilhelm Frick. After Blomberg cane Graf Schwerin von Krosigk, Finance; Alfred Hugenberg, Economics and Food; Franz Seldte, Labour; Freiherr Eltz von Rübenach, Posts and Transport and, as the last, Hermann Göring, First Minister without Portfolio but Prussian Interior Minister. The conservative section of this first Hitler-Cabinet melted quickly. First to resign was Hugenberg (27 June 1933). Papen lasted into 1934, Eltz von Rübenach until 30 January 1937. Neurath was replaced during the Fritsch crisis of February 1938. Only Seldte and Schwerin von Krosigk lasted to the end (and were in the Dönitz government which succeeded Hitler). Blomberg, by far the most important of them, had to resign in 1936 for having not mentioned to Hitler that his new bride had been a prostitute. Until 1934 he persistently refused pressure from Röhm to combine the Reichswehr and SA into a single force.

CHAPTER 13

Six Million Unemployed

This was round figures. According to the painstaking official statisticians, 6,013,000 were unemployed at the end of January 1933. On 15 February 1933 the number had increased to a peak of 6,047,000, then began to fall slowly. In March it was little over 5,500,000 and by the end of May five million. This decompression was naturally felt amongst the SA unemployed. It was they who had not only put their time at the disposition of the party now in government, but had often jeopardized their own lives, without the expectation of any return, and had never asked for any reward. That they should now have priority when the new jobs were handed out was understood by employers now trying to gain the affection of the new government. Marxist militants and 'non-Aryans' were less sought after for the workplace.

The SA and the German people as a whole sighed with relief. In the first elections held in the Third Reich on 5 March 1933, the NSDAP increased its share of the vote from 11 million to 17 million. This gave them 43.9 per cent of the Reichstag seats, or 284 of the 647 available, a proportion never previously obtained in German parliamentary history by one party. Adding to this the 52 seats of the DNVP, the Bad Harzburg coalition had an absolute majority of 25. The Marxist representation shrank: the Communist KPD lost 19 seats to finish with 81. Equally striking was the turnout of 88.8 per cent of those entitled to vote, the highest ever recorded either in the Imperial or Weimar periods.

From my own experience I can confirm the general spirit abroad amongst the people: it was the sensation of enormous confidence in finally recovering our national self-esteem after long years of misery and disorder. A people with a cultural, intellectual and work tradition such as ours in the heart of Europe deserved nothing less. The new Interior Minister, Dr Wilhelm Frick (1877–1946, executed at Nuremberg), was no doubt right when he said the day after the elections: 'The German people have given Adolf Hitler charge of the government in a demonstration of unparalleled confidence, to bring about within four years the economic recovery of this country.'

Personally I did not vote for the NSDAP in March 1933. I was enfranchised and absolutely determined not to miss the opportunity to express my will through the ballot box. A bet amongst democratic novices ruined my intention. We were a group with diverse political leanings, and while discussing the coming election a heated discussion developed. Adversaries of National Socialism were of the opinion that the elections were a farce. For that reason the 'Nazis' had burned down the Reichstag and the opposition press (still independent) was for some reason lying about it: The 'Decree for Defence of Volk and State' signed the day after the Reichstag fire had removed all basic rights and opened the gates for whatever arbitrary procedures were required. Those sympathetic to Nazism, such as I, protested; no political party had yet been banned, not even the Communists, despite the fact that the Dutch national van der Lubbe, who confessed to having set the fire, was a Communist. In the coming elections everybody could vote for whichever party they pleased. 'Then vote KPD!' one of my companions smirked, 'and then we shall see what happens to you.' I held out my hand. 'A deal. I shall vote Communist, but Hitler will still win.' I was right. Nothing happened to me. The secret ballot was zealously protected in the Third Reich. In its lifetime nobody ever asked me when and where I voted, for whom, for what and why.

The Nazis might not have cared, but this changed after we lost the war and the victors wanted to teach us 'democracy'. For this purpose they had us fill out a form with 129 questions, amongst them: 'During the Hitler years, when and where did you vote, for whom and why?'

During 1933, the SA had little to do. The immediate task was to process the enormous quantity of applications to join the organization. This was a lot of work. Less burdensome was the day when they had to guard the Jewish businesses after international Jewry declared war on Germany through an article in the London *Daily Express* on 24 March 1933. Across the width of the front page the title read: 'Judea Declares War on Germany'. The long, detailed article explained *inter alia* that 'fourteen million Jews scattered across the world are united as one man'.[*] The reply to this declaration of war was delayed until 1 April 1933 when SA men new and old were stationed in front of Jewish businesses holding mass-produced placards reading: '*Deutsche! Wehrt Euch gegen die judische Greuel Propaganda. Kauft nur bei Deutschen!*'[†] It was a reply more symbolic than anything else, and the effort probably had no effect on community work.

SA men who could not be reintegrated at once into the workforce after the democratic seizure of power began to whisper of 'a second revolution'. It would be 'national', but more than ever 'social'. Röhm could count on the support of the majority when he said in a speech on 18 April 1934: 'We' – and by 'we' he meant the SA and himself – 'did not make a national revolution but a National Socialist revolution, with special attention to the socialist factor', and he continued by saying that he would not be disposed to abandon any part of the 'socialist' intentions. Reaction and revolution were two deadly enemies. Better it would have been to have skimmed off

[*] Erich Kern, *Verheimlichte Dokumente*, Buenos Aires, 1988.
[†] 'Germans! Protect yourselves against Jewish atrocity propaganda. Buy only from Germans!'

the reactionaries from the SA ranks than attempt to integrate them. 'But we shall break their necks without pity if they attempt to act as reactionaries,' he promised.

These are the typical words of an old warrior whose rule of life was 'always be hard'. He was a stimulant for his men, but for the political class at whom he was aiming his words it was a cold shower. Prudent observers of the time, including amongst others Heinrich Bennecke, thought that these very words sparked off the sequence of events which two months later would culminate in the Bad Wiessee tragedy in which Röhm himself and other senior SA commanders would be the victims.

Bennecke pointed out that during the months when Röhm was sharpening his knives, unemployment in Germany played a key role in all the major political problems.[*] Difficult social problems plagued the hundreds of thousands of SA unemployed. Evidently – with the best intentions – Röhm wanted to popularize the slogan 'Second Revolution'.

On 6 June 1933 Hitler had summoned all Gauleiters to the Reich Chancellery to warn them expressly that 'the revolution is not a permanent situation, it cannot be installed so as to last for ever. It is necessary to steer the revolution to the state of evolution.'[†] A little before, Röhm had called himself 'more Papist than the Pope', as Jordan reported, and continued: 'The SA is not going to allow the revolution to sleep, or be betrayed halfway down the road ... the brown army is the nation's last reserve.'

What conditions Hitler propounded to Röhm respecting German military reactivation when he summoned him from Bolivia on the threshold of seizing power are unknown. Bennecke suggests that Hitler may have insinuated that it would be possible to integrate the SA into the Reichswehr as a means of pepping it up. There is concrete evidence for this. For example, all pre-military training was given over to the SA. On

[*] Bennecke, *Hitler*.
[†] *Völkischer Beobachter*, 8 July 1933.

19 July 1933 a senior SA commander, SA General Krüger, took charge of the administrative council for the strengthening of youth inherited from the Weimar Republic and this was undoubtedly an institution to train and harden German youth on a military basis. He received military directives and financial means from the Reichswehr, which is to say from the appropriate minister, who was Blomberg. Röhm, who cherished the hope of occupying this office himself, received the appointment of minister without portfolio as a consolation on 1 December 1933.

Equally many veteran former Army officers, who abounded in the SA, were disappointed. They and hundreds of thousands of unemployed SA men from the most varied backgrounds were the ferment for the second revolution, the one they called 'The Real One'.

Much later Hitler reined back their ambitions. The Reichswehr, or Wehrmacht as it was renamed after the death of President von Hindenburg and the oath sworn to the 'Führer and Reich Chancellor', was untouchable. According to the constitution, which Adolf Hitler had sworn on oath to uphold – and we must not forget that he took power in a totally legal way through a majority of the votes cast – the Commander-in-Chief of the German armed forces was not the Chancellor, a former Army private, but President von Hindenburg. He had been honoured with the rank of field marshal as a hero of the Great War, and it was to him that Hitler had sworn loyalty at Potsdam Cathedral, black top hat in hand and with a clear bow of reverence as he shook the hand which the President offered him. More still: he had given his word to the President when asked to form a new government, and at the request of Hindenburg's military entourage, principally Blomberg, an undertaking not to embroil the Reichswehr in politics in any respect. To a certain extent it was a repetition of the oath he had sworn to the courts in 1924 to take power only by legal means.

Adolf Hitler accepted the risk of an SA simmering on a stove lit with the fire of unemployment. On New Year's Eve 1933 he had written to the SA leader a letter of thanks calling the victory of 30 January 1933 'something for which in the first place you take the credit', and rounded off 'with warm friendship and grateful recognition for the unforgettable services you rendered to the National Socialist Movement and the German people'. These words, written by the most important man in the country, possibly went to Röhm's head. He had not come out of his stupor by 28 February 1934 when Hitler expounded his programme to the senior Reichswehr and SA commanders saying, and leaving no room for doubt, that the role of the SA was the pre- and post-military training of future Army men only.

Hitler did not wish his governmental programme to be ruined by the hare-brained ambitions of a few subordinates. A fortnight before 30 June 1934 at Tempelhof airport after returning from a visit to Mussolini: 'By all this talk of a "second revolution", the SA is separating itself from me in all reasonable elements . . . . I am not a Lenin. What I want is order.' He could have added: 'and less a Trotsky, who failed with the blunder of the "permanent revolution"'.

Hitler knew from the day he took power that the key to overcoming problems with the SA was the elimination of unemployment. For this reason he dug the first symbolic spit of earth with a spade to commence the net of autobahns designed by himself. That was on 29 September 1933. Some 16,000 kilometres were planned, of which 3,000 had been finished by 1938. Hundreds of thousands of men found work on the project. It was the precondition for starting up Volkswagen production, begun the same year on the basis of conversations with the winning designer Friedrich Porsche (1875–1951) and Hitler's sketches. Mass production (with financial help from the Arbeitsfront) began before the Second World War started, but could not satisfy public demand because of the unexpected military necessities. I was unable to obtain the VW I ordered despite my good salary at the Scherl publishing house and my appointment as a war correspondent in Spain, but finally I got the deposit back and used it later to buy a Fiat Topolino. I never used it much because in August 1939 I was drafted to an Army propaganda company and in the course of the war gave up my tiny car for a panzer.

Volkswagen and the autobahns were two of the many tools used to eradicate unemployment. It was the primary objective of the government to eliminate that national cancer using enormous efforts, and not to provoke war as is alleged and believed today. The more the intolerable pressure on the six million disappeared, the greater was the optimism of SA men young and old. Talk about the 'second revolution' was gradually disappearing, and the misery of six million men and women and their families decreasing. This was the most important thing of all.

CHAPTER 14

A Reich without Hitler?

What might appear to be an absurdity too doubtful even for contemporary re-educationalist historians to credit came to light in a 1993 book, published sixty years after the dawn of the Third Reich with the collaboration of no lesser authorities than the Koblenz Central Archive, the Berlin Document Centre and the Institute for Contemporary History (IfZ) Munich. Its title is *The Gerlich–Bell Secret File.*[*]

Fritz Gerlich (b. 1883) began his career as a journalist in the advertising department of the magazine *Kathreiners Kaffee-Ersatz*, not a promising starting point for a high-flying career in journalism. During the brief period of Bolshevik terror in Munich, he fled with Hoffmann's Bavarian government to Bamberg to support the coup of separatist Kahr in Bavaria. He published a weekly, *The Right Path*, with no great circulation, which was opposed to the rise of Hitler. On 31 June 1932, the day of the sensational NSDAP electoral victory when the Party won 230 seats and became the strongest group, Gerlich's magazine commented: 'National Socialism is a pest.' Six months later Adolf Hitler was Chancellor and the demands of the Nationalist daily *München-Augsburger Abendzeitung*: '*The Right Path* is a poisonous serpent whose head must be crushed' were soon met. Its last edition appeared on 8 March 1933. Five days later Goebbels was appointed Minister of Propaganda. There were no more insults from *The Right Path*, which had been turned into 'an unpaved byway'. Nothing befell the editor

* Hans-Günter Ricardi/Klaus Schumann, *Geheimakte Gerlich/Bell*, Munich, 1993.

and director, however. The supplier of venom was Georg Bell, a shadowy individual of whom nothing much is known except that he worked for the British secret service. He was the son of a wealthy Nuremberg family, born in 1898, and the surname had passed from a Scots ancestor. He took part in the First World War from early on and was an enthusiast of Brigade *Erhardt*, whose members wore the swastika on their helmets. He supported the Kapp coup in 1920 in Berlin, ran with Hitler and finally joined the NSDAP, receiving the relatively low Party number 290,055. Already in that epoch he knew Party member Hauptmann Ernst Röhm on the extreme right of the political spectrum of the new Weimar Republic, but he did not attach much importance to the 'king of the Bavarian machine gun'. In November 1930, almost ten years after their first meeting, they began to meet frequently.

It is no secret that Röhm spoke of 'private Hitler' during the postwar period they spent together. Hitler was the 'drummer boy' whose services would be very useful at the dawn of the Party, but he would then have to be supplemented and the Party brought to final effectiveness by Röhm's own political authority. The book just referred to draws attention to another book quoting Röhm who in 1922 praised 'the unquestioned motivation of Hitler' who travelled the land 'with light luggage' but whose vision did not extend 'beyond the German borders. We will side-line him in time.'[*]

Röhm knew of Bell's contacts abroad and made a formal pact with him. This took place at Röhm's home in Munich on 21 April 1931 at three in the afternoon in the presence of Röhm's adjutant, SA General Dr Karl Leon Graf du Moulin-Eckart. The contract set out in detail Bell's duties and remuneration: a modest salary of 350 RM and victuals. The deal was signed with a handshake and a word of honour. Röhm observed: 'You realize that from now on we shall have to be

---

[*] Ricardi, *Hitler und seine Hintermänner*. Munich, 1991.

united as one flesh.' Bell went on to say that Röhm understood 'I will succeed or fall alongside him.' Both would fall.

A few days before the formal contract, on 15 April 1931 Röhm wrote to Bell, making reference to the need for Bell to travel: 'Dear Bell, you have to do something for me ... '* He could present himself calmly as Röhm's 'man of confidence' because 'we have a major advantage in that Britain knows the truth about us,' Röhm said. The ideas which Bell was to put forward both in London and Paris about Röhm's foreign politics were set out in close detail in a nine-page memorandum delivered to Bell by adjutant Moulin-Eckart. The striking omission from this document is the name Adolf Hitler, which never appears.

The SA is not 'an army for future vengeance or something similar, but exists only to defend the Party and guarantee its functioning as well as propagate its ideas'. The primary purpose which Röhm is pursuing is 'European reconciliation'. The attempted reconciliation with the Soviet Union is 'rejected outright', contrary to the current policy of the Foreign Ministry and the Defence Ministry of the Weimar Republic. Its (Röhm's) final aim is the 'fortification of Europe'. For this reason he considers that 'it is in the interests not only of Germany but of all Europe that the European nations unite in a determined manner'. Röhm believes that in this endeavour 'Germany is the leading country' and for that reason 'the social ideal of a strong Germany would be Great Britain'. The idea of a union between the world's leading naval power and the greatest territorial potential of Europe – 'even today' – would be enough 'to recognize the advantages of such a combination'. The promising document concluded by saying: 'The stabilization of the world would be assured.' The role which the flamboyant Röhm had assigned to his agent Bell coincided almost word for word with the concepts which Adolf Hitler held regarding foreign policy.

* Document 403/SA, Berlin Document Centre.

It had been gone into extensively in the meeting they had on 5 March 1931.

The SA did not lack men prepared to invest their strength, capabilities and even their lives to ensure the success of National Socialist ideas. What they totally lacked was money. The contributions of the Party exchequer, administered con-scientiously by Franz Xavier Schwarz (died of malnutrition in a US death camp on German soil) were minute. The report of the SA leadership office states laconically: 'Financially the SA can go no further.' This was no exaggeration. Document 403/SA at the Berlin Document Centre has a statement by Röhm dated 9 June 1931: 'The urgent economic situation calls for immediate and radical measures.' Bell promised to remedy the extreme poverty.

Röhm had other plans to pursue with Bell. His intention was to 'neutralize the NSDAP leadership' and take it over himself with the help of the SA. Röhm really believed himself more capable than Hitler, and considered his colleague incompetent. For this reason he wanted to prepare the SA to take personal and material command of the Nazi Party, and soon he was creating administrative departments in his general staff to cover the broadest range of interests, none of which had anything to with the specific obligations of a defence organization.

Much later Bell described the orders given him by Röhm:

The duties and responsibilities which were imposed on me by Röhm as the basis of his planning were to concentrate on structuring the SA in such a way that it could exist independent of the Party and moreover transform itself into its own Party and so separate out its present politicians whom Röhm classified as pure demagogues. To achieve this I would have to arrange to set up and expand a large-scale SA spy network at home and abroad; create an SA Press office and a newspaper, *Der SA-Mann*; establish a propaganda office for Röhm personally and the SA, at home and abroad, and collect money for these aims, and channel into the SA treasury those funds currently flowing from industry to the Party.[*]

Bell also attempted to obtain money from abroad. In May 1931 he advised Röhm of the conditions to obtain unlimited credit being proposed by British and French financial circles interested in gaining influence in the NSDAP: these conditions requiring that within two to three months Röhm had to assume absolute command of the NSDAP; the German Press would have to accept British influence; an office would be created for pre-determined foreign policies; and a military office would be created to handle the question of defence in a manner to be agreed upon. 'I informed Röhm of this in detail.'

Bell noted the outcome of this conversation as follows: 'On 29 May 1931 after consulting Röhm I informed London and Paris that he accepted the conditions and would attempt to comply.' This seems to be a peculiar concept of 'loyalty'. Another financial suggestion for Bell came from the oil magnate Sir Henry Deterding. A Dutch national, he had pro-German sympathies. In 1907 he had merged his Royal Dutch Petroleum Company with the British company Shell to create the Royal Dutch Shell consortium. In 1920 he received a knighthood and British citizenship. The Bolshevist Revolution had deprived him of his oil wells in the Caucasus and he was therefore an enemy of the Soviet regime.

In exchange for a future financial package from Deterding, Röhm had to commit himself to grant Royal Dutch Shell privileged status in the event that the National Socialist Party should come to power in Germany under him. This agreement was never confirmed. To give Röhm liberty of action he worked out a plan with his entourage in 1931. This was a

---

[*] Nikolaus von Preradovich, *30 Juni 1934*, Rosenheim, 1934.

conspiracy to murder Hitler by shooting him. Lots were drawn and the would-be assassin was SA Standartenführer Julius Uhl, adviser to Röhm and a little later commander of the armed guard protecting Röhm's SA general staff. Bell was informed of all this.

The assassination attempt was frustrated by leaks to Party circles which prompted an investigation. At first nothing was uncovered. Because Bell could not obtain the funds which Röhm was counting on, and he was not being paid properly or punctually, and his expenses were not being reimbursed, he resigned from the NSDAP on 8 October 1932 and from that moment set out to gather any information prejudicial to the National Socialist Movement for passing to Gerlich and publication in *The Right Path*.

After the NSDAP was elected to power, Bell sought refuge in the Austrian Tyrol. Röhm set out to kill him since Bell was a dangerous witness to the assassination plot. As part and parcel of the investigation of the 1931 rumours, Bell was also being sought by Heydrich's SD through the Munich police. Bell's whereabouts were discovered, and when an SS and SD squad departed from Munich to pick him up, Julius Uhl inveigled himself into the group without attracting attention. After a long conversation in the small hotel where Bell was staying, the suspect agreed to accompany the police group back to Munich and make a statement. At that moment Uhl drew a gun from his pocket and shot Bell dead. In this way the plot to kill Hitler could not be proven. Röhm was unable to supplant Hitler, nor push him aside so as to create 'a Reich without Hitler'. Neither had Gerlich and Bell been able to prevent the Weimar Republic yielding power to the NSDAP on 30 January 1933.

CHAPTER 15

'I am Going to Destroy You'

On 7 June 1934 the official German Government Press Office announced that Minister Röhm was to take 'a holiday of several weeks duration on medical advice'.* Next day Röhm spoke in person 'anticipating erroneous interpretations'. He was taking a holiday to recover from a painful nervous condition. Part of his SA was also taking leave in June, but the majority would go in July 'because the SA would require all our men's strength and energy'. At the same time he warned, 'There are enemies who hope that after the holidays many men will not return to our ranks. We hope they comfort themselves with that notion. At the right time they will receive a fitting response.' He added, 'The SA is, and will continue to be, Germany's destiny.' The proclamation is signed, 'The Chief of the SA General Staff, Röhm'.†

Four days before sending the SA on leave, Röhm had a meeting with Hitler at the Chancellery behind closed doors. It is assumed that they spoke about the political course Röhm was steering; he had expected substantial personnel changes after the seizure of power, particularly the removal of 'bureaucrats and reactionaries' – both within and outside the NSDAP – and

---

* Höhne, *Mordsache Röhm*, p. 229: Preradovich, *30 Juni 1934*, p. 16.

† The document states that the SA would serve '*Volk und Vaterland*' and not '*Reich und Führer*' as had then become the common terminology. He also did not finish off with the customary '*Heil Hitler!*' Christa Schroeder, *Er war mein Chef*, Herbig, 1985/2004, p. 52.

the filling of the vacant posts by SA men and true National Socialist Party members, whom he had in mind but did not list by name.

At the beginning of 1933, Röhm had said:

An enormous victory has been achieved, but not the final and total victory. It was not the deeds of 30 January in themselves which shaped the German National Socialist revolution. Those who only wanted to take part in magnificent marches with glittering torches, beating drums and deafening bass drums, to march behind flaring banners and colourful standards and now believe this was a revolution, they can go home. They confuse the 'national uprising' for 'revolution'. Therefore I say to them, to those who are suddenly Party members or sympathizers, and who quickly took their seats in the new Germany – if they were not already seated beforehand – believing that all is now done and we are on the right track, and that we have had enough of revolution and now we have to get back to normal, to those I say clearly: there is a long way to go to reach that goal, and while the true National Socialist Germany awaits its fulfilment, the passionate struggle of the SA and SS has not finished. Therefore the SA and SS will not allow the revolution to sleep or be betrayed along the road by those who never fought for it … if bureaucratic souls believe it enough for the state apparatus just to change its emblem, and consider that the revolution has gone on long enough, then yes, in that case we will say that they are right: it really is time that the national revolution finished and transformed itself into a National Socialist revolution. Whether they like it or not, we shall carry on with our struggle. We shall carry on until at the end they understand that it means going on with them, of if they do not like it, without them, and if it becomes necessary, against them.[*]

* Preradovich, p. 11

A little afterwards he warned: 'The new regime handled the representatives of the previous system with incomprehensible gentleness after taking over. NSDAP politicians will have to disappear. Those people were necessary to achieve the first goal, but now they are a burden. We have to get rid of them quickly. Then one can begin the real revolution.'[*] The result of this true, or as they said, second revolution, must be an SA state. The fight against bureaucracy, the Party bosses, against the charlatans and bourgeoisie was geared up totally to Röhm's nature. For him, apparently, there were revolutionaries, and those who were not, and he had no doubt to which category he belonged. His last and most important goal was to fuse the SA and Reichswehr, merging both institutions into a militant organization under his own command. He had the hope that a kind of 'popular Army' could be achieved with a special efficiency. SA chiefs would run it and their lack of military know-how would be compensated 'with well-versed General Staff officers placed at their side'.[†]

Röhm's plans were aimed at the experts in administration and industry who had already contributed much to resolving the economic crisis, the loss of whom would endanger the completion of the work. They were also aimed at the NSDAP leaders and the military officer corps. Hitler, who in contrast to Röhm had declared that the revolution was completed, rejected all these demands out of hand and issued the SA rebels with dire warnings. In particular he underlined the fact that Germany needed for the future an Army based on conscription and led by professional soldiers, because a militia composed of precariously trained soldiers would not meet the demands of modern warfare. A defensive structure like that of Switzerland, which had an ideal topography for defence, would be catastrophic for Germany, open on all borders and with neighbours keen to expand. For this reason Hitler rejected the

[*] Ibid.
[†] Höhne, p. 174f.

idea of a popular militia with the words, 'It is my firm decision that the future Army will be motorized. Whoever intends to oppose this, my decision, I shall destroy that man.' The Supreme Commander of the Reichswehr was President von Hindenburg, and he was also opposed in principle to Röhm's ideas. Hitler had assured the President that the Army and its structure were inviolate. In a letter to Röhm at the end of 1933, Hitler set out his guidelines: 'The Army is to defend the nation against external attack: the duty of the SA is to guarantee the internal victory of National Socialism.'* Accordingly Röhm had no jurisdiction to meddle in military affairs. On 28 February 1934 he had to sign an agreement that the Reichswehr was responsible for the external defence of the country, and the SA only for pre- and post-military training of the men in accordance with the outlines fixed by the Reichswehr Ministry.

Röhm ventured to assert, with regard to this agreement, 'It is a new Treaty of Versailles,' as he told a group of SA commanders. 'Hitler, if only we could rid ourselves of him!' And regarding Hitler's demand that discord between the Reichswehr and SA be avoided, he said: 'What this ridiculous private says does not apply to us. Hitler is not loyal, and the least he deserves is a prolonged vacation. If we cannot achieve things with Hitler, we shall get them without him.'† What would happen after 'the least he deserves ... ' he did not say, but in line with the way he had planned to kill Hitler in 1931 while speaking of his loyalty, in 1934 he was also pledging his loyalty while wanting to 'do things without him'. For example, Röhm declared in his traditional Order of the Day on Hitler's birthday in 1934 that Hitler had made reality the 2,000-year-old German dream to 'create a united nation, above the social, class and religious differences'. At the same time Röhm was renewing the oath of his 'brown and black battalions, the SA and SS' for blind obedience and loyalty.

* Höhne, p. 173.
† Höhne, p. 206

From the spring of 1934 Röhm began to repeat his demands with growing insistence despite Hitler's contradicting him and threatening: 'Whoever challenges the authority of the state will be punished severely irrespective of the office he holds',[*] and shortly before 30 June 1934 in a radio broadcast, Rudolf Hess prepared the way:

> Only the orders of the Führer, to whom we have sworn loyalty, carry weight. Woe be to them who disobey those orders believing they are providing thereby a service to the revolution. Miserable beings who think themselves chosen to help the Führer from below by availing themselves of agitation they consider revolutionary. Adolf Hitler is a revolutionary of the very highest level and needs no crutches. Woe be to them who tread clumsily in the fine weft of his strategic plans, thinking they can speed them up. Whoever does so will be an enemy of the revolution even when he acts with the best intentions. The enemies of modern Germany try to fight us with arguments similar to our own, and what they baptize with the name 'second revolution' is nothing else but a revolt against National Socialism.

Next day Hermann Göring issued a statement no less clear: 'If a fine day comes to burst the dam it will be I who delivers the blow.' He went on to speak of the confidence that the young National Socialist Movement had discovered in the German people: 'Whoever strikes out against that confidence risks his head.' And the same went for all the rest. A part of the SA began to arm and demonstrate, and not a few of its leaders were saying that if it came to it, they would achieve their aims by force. Soon it was not possible to decide if what they were saying and demonstrating about was being done solely to bring pressure on Hitler, or if they actually were preparing an armed confrontation. Röhm's agitation was finding fertile soil,

---

[*] Gerd Rühle, *Das Dritte Reich*, 2nd Year, Berlin, 1934, p. 231.

principally amongst those men who, despite the general economic progress nationally, had still not been able to find work.

It had been relatively easy, within a brief time of taking power, to employ and pay those unemployed who had entered the SA before 30 January 1933. Röhm, however, had enlarged the organization after that date to such an extent that its growth far exceeded the economic expansion. Moreover he was ignoring the rule that nobody could enter the SA who was not already a member of the Nazi Party. The Party had closed its registers to new entrants in conformity with a principle laid down by Hitler in *Mein Kampf*: 'It is extremely dangerous for a political movement to grow extremely rapidly.'* Those un-worthy of membership and cowards could infiltrate with ease, and in due course form a majority to undermine the organiz-ation and use it for their own selfish motives. Röhm rejected this line of reasoning and, on the contrary, took aboard any-body who came forth simply to swell the numbers. His intention was to create a gigantic organization to realize his personal and political agenda. Whole units of the Fighting League of the Red Front transferred into the SA. They were known ironically as the 'Beefsteak Companies': brown outside, red inside. Many of these placements could not unhitch their Communist sentiments, and fell in enthusiastically behind Röhm for the 'second revolution'.

Under the constitution of the Weimar Republic, the President had the power to appoint and remove the Chancellor and his ministers; he could also declare a state of emergency and transfer executive power to the Reichswehr. Until the day of Hindenburg's death on 2 August 1934, Adolf Hitler had to keep this presidential power in mind, and knew he could be relieved of his office if his policies were not to Hindenburg's liking. It was precisely this which a group close to Hindenburg wanted.

* Hitler, *Mein Kampf*, p. 656.

Their spokesman was Vice-Chancellor Franz von Papen. In 1933 he had made a decisive contribution to the success of the NSDAP in the hope of being able to control the policies of the Third Reich through a non-National Socialist government – thus Hitler's government at the outset held only three National Socialists, including Hitler, out of ten cabinet members.

When he saw that his planning was coming undone, Papen and some of his collaborators set out to paralyze the NSDAP by having the President declare a state of emergency. The best way to achieve this was through Röhm's plans and to highlight the conduct of the SA, frequently undisciplined, which Röhm left unpunished. The idea behind all this was the age and ailing health of the President, whose approaching death could be predicted with certainty. Understanding this purpose, Hitler, Interior Minister Frick, Hess and SA General Lütze attempted to influence Röhm to moderate his ambitions. The warnings, rather than pacifying Röhm, spurred him on; his threats against 'the enemies of the SA' became more strident day by day. Rebellious groups within his organization began to consider themselves betrayed by Hitler and were openly declaring their readiness to impose their ideas by force. In that climate they started to act against the Reichswehr, which in turn unleashed counter-measures in military quarters. In the face of this escalation of the tension between the Reichswehr and SA, amidst rumour and suspicion, it seemed certain that both sides were gearing up for a major clash.

Since the majority of the SA was being sent on one month's leave from 1 July 1934, and during this time no special occurrences were expected which would justify the conspirators asking the President for a state of emergency, they decided to act earlier to achieve their ends. On 17 June 1934, Papen spoke at Marburg, criticizing the NSDAP severely, hoping that the resultant controversy might provide sufficient motivation for a complaint to the President and so engineer the removal of the

Hitler government, and the transfer of executive power into the hands of the Reichswehr.

Papen and his collaborators decided to visit the aged President at his estate in East Prussia on 30 June, having prepared an extensive complaint against the SA, and convinced that they would not return to Berlin empty-handed, all the more so because Hindenburg did not grasp everything on account of his age (87 years). Hitler had to prevent the visit and do something about Röhm. A part of the SA was arming, fired up by the speeches of Röhm and other SA commanders. They assaulted Reichswehr transports, dug ditches, drew up lists of 'enemies in the SA', prepared holding camps for future detainees and demonstrated in the streets. By the end of June it could not be determined what originated directly from Röhm and his staff, and what was the result of what he had instigated. Since an SA coup seemed imminent and Papen would certainly refer to this to demand the state of emergency, Hitler saw that he had no choice but to take the most drastic action.

Accordingly, though not sure how he was going to resolve his difficulties, he arranged to meet the leaders of the SA conspiracy on 30 June 1934 at the venue where Röhm was spending his leave, the town of Bad Wiessee south of Munich. When Hitler landed at Munich in the early hours of 30 June and discovered that a few hours previously SA leaders had organized a demonstration against him, he felt certain that this was a revolt ordered by Röhm. He told his entourage, 'The traitors are preparing the last test for me. Today at 0200 the Munich SA was alerted and formed up under arms in front of the Feld-herrnhalle. I shall not wait until eleven. I have to act immediately.' Convinced that he had no more time to lose, he travelled to Bad Wiessee without an escort and accompanied only by a few SS men and police, Rudolf Hess, Lütze, Goebbels, and an employee of the SA HQ at Munich. Röhm and six men with him were arrested. Julius Uhl, who was to have murdered

Hitler in 1931, and later killed Bell, was also taken into custody. When they interrogated him on 30 June, he regretted not having a gun on his person at that moment, for if he had he would certainly have shot Hitler with it. Before his execution he revealed his earlier plan to kill Hitler, thus enabling the information to be announced to the Reichstag on 14 July 1934.

The Bad Wiessee incident was unplanned and the measures taken so improvised that even for the transport of the detainees to Stadelheim Prison at Munich a private coach had to be hired. The presence of Dr Goebbels was less a demonstration of confidence than a precautionary measure to watch him at first hand, since he was generally involved in all the revolutionary machinations of the Party to some degree. Convinced of the need to avoid a mutiny inside the SA, Hitler had Röhm and some of his close colleagues shot. He told the Reichstag that it was the bitterest measure he had ever taken. That same day he put Papen under house arrest to prevent his seeing the President. Some of Papen's collaborators were also shot, amongst them Edgar Julius Jung, who had written Papen's speech at Marburg and had been thinking about assassinating Hitler; nothing had come of this because he wanted to be the new Reich Chancellor and the philosopher Leopold Ziegler advised him not to become a murderer if he intended to assume high office in government. For that reason Jung had decided to help unseat Hitler by the state of emergency tactic.

Papen resigned as Vice-Chancellor, and was appointed German ambassador to Vienna a few weeks later. In explanation afterwards he said that he had not had the intention to mutiny, and the revolt had been a misinterpretation of something he did which induced many SA men in numerous operations to act in the manner alleged. What Röhm wanted was to give the 'enemies of the SA' a 'fitting response' at some future time, which did not mean give in to their plans. Without any doubt he created the conditions for 30 June 1934, but what was avoided that day was not sedition by Röhm, but sedition by Franz von Papen. If the Vice-Chancellor had not instigated the conflict with premeditation and attempted to use it for his own ends, the problems provoked by Röhm would almost certainly have been resolved in another manner. The death of President von Hindenburg on 2 August 1934 eliminated the fear of a state of emergency and with it the transfer of power to the Reichswehr. Without doubt Hitler could have found a compromise with Röhm without bloodshed, for the men of the SA, restless on account of unemployment, were being fed so rapidly into employment that soon they would lack the incentive to want a 'second revolution'.

The intervention against the seditious SA leaders was accepted by the majority of the German people and by many SA men who rejected the ideas of the minority around Röhm who wanted the 'second revolution'. The state administrative apparatus was no longer jammed up by Röhm's minions, and the Reichswehr could now prepare for German rearmament, reintroducing conscription without impediment. Hitler kept his word, expressed clearly and repeatedly to Röhm, that he would not interfere in the Reichswehr structure. The future Feldmarschall von Reichenau explained Hitler's attitude to a French journalist: 'The Chancellor kept his word that he would extinguish the fires lit by Röhm when the latter was attempting to merge the SA and Reichswehr ... the Army admires him for his personal valour, and I repeat the words he said recently, "The Reichswehr can trust in me, and I trust in it."'

Hitler wrote to the new SA Chief of Staff: 'My dear SA-Chief Lütze, It is my desire that the SA is structured as a loyal and strong body of the National Socialist Movement. Imbued with obedience and blind discipline, it will help in the education and formation of the New Man.'* In his speech of 13 July 1934, he assured the Reichstag that the SA, now severed from Röhm's

---

* *Dokumente der deutschen Politik*, in *Der Aufbau des deutschen Führerstaates*, 5th edition, Berlin, 1939, p. 49.

leadership, deserved a renewal of his total confidence. A few days after 30 June 1934, the SS became independent of the Nazi Party, and from then on, Hitler was accompanied during the memorial services for the fallen and the Nazi Party rallies on the Luitpoldhain at Nuremberg not only by SA chief Viktor Lütze, but also by SS leader Heinrich Himmler.

CHAPTER 16

The Fate of Some National Socialists

During my research for this book, I had conversations over the years with several former high-ranking SA men who not only survived 30 June 1934 and the Second World War but also the vengeful tribunals of the victors. I am indebted to them for important references, documents and historical notes about the SA as well as valuable accounts of their own experiences, impressions and points of view – at times contradictory – as ex-activists of the Movement.

The last of them, Erhard von Schmidt, died on 27 January 1994 during the writing of this book, at the age of 91. During the Great War a cadet at Berlin-Lichterfelde, he lived through the painful parturition of the Weimar Republic, found his way to the NSDAP in the confused years before 1933, and endured another world war together with its consequences, lived through and for Germany. Then he waited four decades to see if he could find another SA soldier able to 'explain the reasons why we became followers of Adolf Hitler'. Schmidt wrote: 'Our generation is dying out. Soon they will be all gone.' For this reason he gave me his notes and documents in evidential proof. These have been of fundamental importance for me, above all those relating to 30 June 1934, because I had only been able to look on 'from outside' as an ex-SA man.

Erhard von Schmidt had joined the SA before 1933 and upon reaching the rank of Standartenführer was given a brigade in Mecklenburg. He got on excellently with the local Gauleiter, mainly because they came from such different backgrounds.

While Schmidt was of the nominal aristocracy, Gauleiter Friedrich Hildebrandt had a Mecklenburg peasant background, a worthy origin he concealed before volunteering for the front, as a Freikorps man and entering the NSDAP in 1925 (membership number 3,653). Later, Hildebrandt was made Gauleiter in his own province and became a Reichstag deputy and was captured in 1945 by the Americans, who murdered him at Landsberg prison in 1948.

Schmidt also knew an authentic general of the First World War, Graf von der Schulenburg, who had won much respect as Chief of Staff in the Army of the Crown Prince, and commander of the Gardes du Corps Regiment at Potsdam. Even before the seizure of power by the National Socialists this officer joined Hitler's brownshirts as an SA Mann. Schulenburg was an enthusiastic National Socialist with five sons. He soon rose to Sturmbannführer in the SA brigade staff commanded by Schmidt from the end of 1933. Both men were of the hereditary nobility and became close on account of their political and professional relationships. Schulenburg talked of his service and of his sons. Of these, the fifth boy, Friedrich Werner, would become embroiled at the centre of a family tragedy twelve years later in connection with the July 1944 plot to kill Hitler. Goebbels kept me informed of these events at the time.

As Goebbels's personal press attaché from 1943 to 1945 I kept a personal diary. My entry for 5 August 1944 states: 'Goebbels told me about a series of family tragedies linked to the events of 20 July. SS General von der Schulenburg [i.e the same SA officer of whom Schmidt had spoken] sent a telegram to the Führer after the attempt congratulating him in emotional words on his miraculous escape. At that moment he was unaware that his own son, the last German ambassador to Moscow, had been one of the ringleaders in the plot. A few days later his second son fell in Normandy. The obituary announcement appeared in the same edition of the *Völkischer*

Beobachter, below the Iron Cross with the swastika at its centre, in which the dishonourable discharge of the other Schulenburg son was reported ... We find ourselves at the limits of two worlds.'*

Rounding off the story, Schmidt recounted that the fifth son had had an excellent diplomatic career in the Third Reich and before that on the management board of the NSDAP, He had been appointed QM-General of the Samland NSDAP in East Prussia, at Fischhausen. His career as an NSDAP executive officer put him in good stead for the other career as a diplomat in the service of the Reich, where he was eventually awarded the very important post of ambassador to Moscow. That lasted until 1941. He took part in the assassination plot of 20 July 1944 and paid for it with his life. His cousin Fritz Dietlof Graf von der Schulenburg is credited in the Resistance literature with having conceived the idea of a 'company of officers' which had the job of arresting Hitler and bringing him to trial or – preferably – shooting him in the event that he resisted.

The tragic history of the von der Schulenburgs brings us too far ahead in the story of the SA. At the beginning of 1934 the SA was still having to cope with a tremendous influx of new members which would bring the total close to four million. There now began the build-up in small steps towards the culminating event in the early summer of that year. Graf von der Schulenburg was of advanced years and held a subordinate rank. Called to the Supreme Command in Munich, he was awarded high honorary rank and given various missions as an advisor within the Mecklenburg SA brigade commanded by Standartenführer von Schmidt. In the course of his duties he informed Schmidt, then scarcely thirty, that he might be transferred soon to Munich. This was important news because Schmidt was planning to marry in July 1934 and settle in the Mecklenburg provincial capital, Schwerin.

* Oven, *Mit Goebbels bis zum Ende*, Vol II, p. 108

Schulenburg also confided to Schmidt that he had mentioned to Röhm his concerns at the tangible rift opening between Röhm and Hitler, and suggested he appoint an officer as mediator. It occurred to him that Schmidt was just the man for the job. Only a few weeks before – possibly May 1934, Schmidt recalled – he had received an 'invitation' – really an order – to take part in a training trip to Weinheim north of Heidelberg at a picturesque spot called Bergstrasse. The participants would be departmental heads of the SA Supreme Command, practically the cream of the SA, some of whom would not survive 30 June 1934. Schmidt mentioned the names of some of those who would be present: SA General (General Staff) Schneidhuber, Ritter von Krausser, Kühme, Hühnlein, Hierl, von der Schulenburg, von Tschammer und Osten, and SA General Schmidt (namesake of the Mecklenburg general).

Röhm took advantage of the opportunity – he never could stop playing at soldiers – to organize a kind of military exercise in the Bergland. The majority of the participants had a very moderate level of military training except for Graf von der Schulenburg with his noteworthy exploits as a general of the General Staff during the Great War. Although Standartenführer von Schmidt had been in uniform in the Great War as a cadet he had not seen action at the front, being only 16, and was taken aback to be given command of a mortar unit, this being a weapon of which he had no knowledge, and one he had never seen before in his life. It seemed that the real purpose of the 'training trip' was to provide Röhm with the opportunity to observe the men of his entourage close to and see how they reacted to daily tests.

Schmidt had a difficult objective. As were all his comrades of similar rank, he was aware of the rumours respecting Röhm's homosexuality. (We simple SA-men had no idea of this at the time, and it never came up in our conversations. Our leaders were men we could trust and wonderful examples of manhood, as far as we were concerned.) Things were different in superior circles. Schmidt had come to Weinheim – according to his version of events – with the secret intention of observing Röhm for any quirks. He arrived at the conclusion that 'as far as I could judge he had none'. The same was thought by his closest colleagues such as Krausser, Schneidhuber and Schmidt (from Munich), all of whom fell victim on 30 June.

During dinner, the only daily meal where everybody met up, Schmidt sat next to Röhm, the idea being to see if he might be an acceptable mediator for the Hitler–Röhm role. The result was positive, according to what Schulenburg told him later in confidence, but the recommendation led nowhere. During the closing festivities of that strange 'training trip' there was a retreat to the terrace of a Heidelberg hotel for a modest dinner, and Schmidt was again placed at Röhm's table. Although there was champagne available 'nobody got drunk,' as Schmidt reported. He concluded his report with an observation that nothing derogatory was said about Hitler 'either by Röhm or any of the senior functionaries, and even less anything mentioned of an intention to revolt'. In May 1934 it seemed that nothing like that existed.

From our SA membership booklet which I had been issued on 1 May 1931, and returned one year later in my immaturity, not having understood correctly Hitler's platform, there is an exhortation of which Schmidt reminded me and which I reproduce here:

Party Member: Never forget you are a defender and representative of the National Socialist Movement and moreover of our cosmic vision. Be for others an example of fearlessness, sacrifice and discipline. As a simple human being be humane, diligent, hard-working and modest. As a leader be harsh with yourself in the fulfilment of your own duties, decisive when necessary, good-hearted and fair with your subordinates, never pedantic in the judgement of human weaknesses, magnanimous in recognizing the needs of others and modest in your own needs.

Recognize in the least of your compatriots your blood-brother, with whom destiny has linked you inseparably, and value the lowest of the road sweepers in your town higher than the king of a foreign country. Never forget that the liberty of your people is the greatest of riches in this world, and remember that the struggle for liberty can never be a war against classes, but only against peoples.

With these words to guide us we were marching away from misery, dishonour and the subjugation prevailing at the beginning of the 1930s and towards a new dawn. These sentiments delighted a comrade of mine of princely blood whom I knew during the Second World War after I joined the Ministry of Propaganda. As ex-members of the NSDAP we were in sympathy and remained in touch after the war. His full name was so long that it needed the full width of the book he gave me as a present with his dedication: Friedrich Christian Prinz zu Schaumburg-Lippe.

Within our ministerial circle we nicknamed this offspring of a princely house, in former times ruling a German region, 'Schaumprinz', 'Prinz' or sometimes the diminutive 'Prinzchen' because of his fragile build. His standing in the SA was very similar to that of Standartenführer Schmidt. In one of his books published postwar he wrote, 'The Party was a formal matter: in the SA I felt at home.' The prince had come to the Party through no less a person than Hitler himself, and he got to Hitler through Rudolf Hess, whom the young prince knew socially in Bad Godesberg at the age of 22. He met Hitler for the first time – it must have been 1928 – in a sparsely furnished little room at Schelling-Strasse 50 in Munich, the original NSDAP headquarters, as he recounts in one of his books.[*]

---

[*] Friedrich Christian Prinz zu Schaumburg-Lippe, *Verdammte Pflicht und Schuldigkeit*, Leoni, 1966.

Adolf Hitler could captivate through his natural affability and long monologues, but he behaved with reserve towards the prince, as the head of a 'workers' party', by deferring to him as 'Your Highness' and said that he could well imagine 'standing down for a monarch', always supposing that he got into power. 'I firmly intend to do that by legal means,' he told the prince.*
Hitler declared himself opposed to all kinds of armed revolutionary attempts or dirty tricks such as were practised by the likes of Strasser, Stennes and Röhm.

'This man was talking to me as a father does to his son,' the prince wrote, and openly admitted that he had the sudden conviction that he should trust Hitler utterly. He was especially impressed by Hitler's eyes, as I was also some time later. Hitler had been blinded temporarily on 14 October 1918 during a poison gas attack; now he radiated a magical force difficult to describe – I would say an hypnotic energy. This must have been what motivated the prince to ask Hitler, at the end of a brief conversation following a monologue, if he might join the Nazi Party. To his surprise and consternation the request was denied, Hitler explaining in detail that the applicant was the prince of a noble dynasty which in former times had reigned over a region of Germany, and he, Hitler, was just the leader of a workers' socialist political party. He requested understanding for his position, and left open the possibility that he would reconsider the request the following year.

They separated in perfect harmony, and the next year the prince joined the Party. He and his wife, Alexandra Gräfin zu Castell-Rüdenhausen, were very frequent guests of Hitler during the years 1933–5, sometimes on repeated occasions in one week or even daily and generally in private, from eight in the evening to two next morning, in Hitler's private apartment. In one of these meetings the prince was introduced to Dr Goebbels who, after being made Minister of Propaganda,

* Ibid.

offered him the post of personal adjutant, which the prince was delighted to accept. He was already at work in his new post when the events of 30 June 1934 occurred.

On that fateful morning, Schaumburg-Lippe was in his office on the Wilhelm-Platz waiting for the return of his minister, who had met the Führer in Bad Godesberg in order to travel together to Bad Wiessee. Suddenly Hermann Göring appeared unannounced. After a formal greeting, Göring went up to the tall windows and, drumming with his fingertips on the pane asked the prince harshly: 'Do you have any idea what is going on today?'* The question was not unjustified, since the prince was not only adjutant to the minister, but also, as SA Sturmführer, one of the adjutants of Karl Ernst, commander of the Berlin-Brandenburg SA. That very day Ernst was to have set off on his honeymoon from Bremerhaven aboard the transatlantic passenger liner *Europa*. Arrested and brought to Berlin, he was shot to death with the words '*Heil Hitler!*' on his lips. Until that moment he had thought it a prank in bad taste.

The prince knew nothing of this. While working with the Minister of Propaganda he was on official leave from the SA. He found Göring's next statement completely incomprehensible: Röhm was to be shot that day. Göring was wrong: Röhm was shot to death on 1 July 1934 at Stadelheim Prison, Munich. During the late afternoon of 30 June when the prince and his wife met Hitler at Goebbels's house, the Führer was wrestling with the problem of what to do about Röhm, who had refused to use the pistol supplied in his cell to shoot himself. Suddenly Hitler turned to the prince, with whom he had enjoyed such a close relationship over recent years, and snapped: 'Where were you today?' and proceeded at once to describe the fate of Karl Ernst, whose honeymoon had met such an abrupt end.

* Friedrich Christian Prinz zu Schaumburg-Lippe, *War Hitler ein Diktator?*, Witten, 1976.

Confused, Schaumburg-Lippe replied, 'In my office working, as usual.' Hitler told him: 'Then you were lucky. If you had been with Ernst, it would have been difficult to have saved you.' In his book, the prince observed: 'This answer gave me the cold shivers.'

CHAPTER 17

Why Weren't You Shot
On 30 June 1934?

This question, stupid as it may sound, was asked in all seriousness of SA General Meinhard Marnitz, in perfect German, by a uniformed sergeant of General Montgomery's staff after the occupation of Kiel. Marnitz was at gunpoint at the time – the victors in conquered Germany in 1945 had a preference for this kind of person as interrogator. Marnitz recounted this episode to me during one of my frequent visits to Germany to research for this book. He died at Eckernförde, at a very advanced age, and was the last of the SA generals.

Marnitz was born on 5 December 1902 at Üxküll, at that time in Livonia, a Baltic province of Russia having Riga as its capital, today split between Estonia and Latvia. He was one of the eleven children of a local Protestant parson. This man was deported and then murdered by the Bolshevists in 1918. Marnitz was sixteen when he volunteered for the Baltic National Defence as a field gunner, and he experienced his baptism of fire at Lake Jägelsee. At the end of the First World War, his mother moved to Treptow on the banks of the River Rega in Pomerania where Meinhard obtained his school-leaving certificate and decided to become a civil engineer. First he worked down the mines at Gutehoffnungshütte. He called this a character-building experience. He had a vision of the world of the 'accursed of the Earth' as the Marxist 'Internationale' called the working masses in the previous century. Gradually he leaned towards National Socialism and through his own experiences gained respect for physical labour. This was the prior step towards his future with a workers' political party, the National Socialists, but he finished his professional training first and obtained his doctorate in engineering at Danzig in 1930.

Nationalism for the young German born abroad was understood. With socialism he had contact in the Ruhr mines. Both merged in the 'logic of *Mein Kampf*'. He was enthused at Hitler's style. Ideas and thoughts held in the minds of millions were expressed in this book in a unique and captivating manner. 'The Racial Community of the People' – 'General Welfare before individual freedom' – 'Blood and Soil': these concepts and many others were put into words by Hitler and made reality. The young engineer decided to join the NSDAP. The landslide election of 14 September 1930 convinced him. It never bothered me that the 'Old Members' should call those who joined the Party after that sensational election 'the autumn opportunists' or even the 'opportunist foxes': criticizing people who made up their minds to take the step when victory seemed within reach, something which – whatever the margin – was not important. To those of us short of voting age these things were irrelevant.

My future superior Joseph Goebbels was not interested in knowing the date of my entry into the NSDAP and SA when I introduced myself, having been sent by OKH (Army High Command) to take up the post of personal press attaché. One fine day a few months before the war ended, he asked me, with a threatening gaze, when I had resigned from both organizations. If I had done so after 6 November 1932 he would have discharged me immediately, even though I had been at his side day and night, on his travels, in his home and wherever he went, because in those elections for the seventh Reichstag session postwar the NSDAP had lost 34 seats, giving rise to fears that support was falling away. Whoever turned his back on the Party at that time could also desert now, when the future of the Reich was a question of life and death. Goebbels's interest in knowing the date when I left the Party came about in the following way.

On 3 August 1944 the last Gauleiters' conference was held. These were always rare occurrences within the complicated governing apparatus of the Third Reich. At this moment, however, Goebbels attributed special importance to it. His adjutant, Schwägermann, and I accompanied him. As usual, I asked if I should wear my uniform as a reserve lieutenant for my role as an OKH war reporter, or civilian dress. He told me to wear a suit. Now I stood out amidst the mixture of brown uniforms, and caught the eye of Martin Mutschmann (1879–1945), Gauleiter of Saxony, to whom I had previously taken a dislike by reason of his opulence, boxer's face and strong Saxon dialect. During a pause in the conference he turned to me and without introducing himself asked in challenging tones: 'Party Member, why are you not wearing your badge in your lapel?' He was referring to a recent instruction which obliged all Party members to wear the badge visibly on their civilian clothing in public, a fact which a growing number were finding inconvenient. I replied to my inquisitioner: 'Because I do not have one, *Herr Gauleiter*. I am not a Party Member.' He asked my name and occupation and advised me with a withering look, 'I shall be complaining to your minister.' And he did. Scarcely had I forgotten this episode – there were more important affairs to worry about in the Ministry – when Goebbels brought up the matter during lunch, which we used to eat in each other's company at table.

'Mutschmann complained about you,' he told me, and went on, 'I like the man as little as you do, especially since I found out confidentially that his wife has been moaning about how the war is going, saying, "Oh Martin, why didn't we stay with the curtains!"' (Mutschmann had founded a successful curtain factory in his native Saxony in 1907, where he became a Gauleiter in 1924.)

'Many of the National Socialist leaders think that the job of Gauleiter is beyond Mutschmann's capabilities. It is not everybody who can adapt to the demands of high office, but even so, Herr von Oven, he should not have handled you like that.' I was asking myself how to put this right while Goebbels was talking, and drumming his fingers on the table-top, one of his habits I knew well. Taking advantage of the pause I told him, 'Herr Minister, I did not intend to offend or mock the Gauleiter. I actually am not a Party Member.'

'What?' His features began to harden. 'I resigned from the Party and SA in 1932 and I declared it in the form I filled out when I was transferred into your ministry.' 'When was this exactly?' he demanded.

'1 May 1932.' He relaxed. 'Wasn't it always the best who abandoned us in those times?' He was referring to Hauptsturmfuhrer Stennes and his revolt, which had been responsible for my joining and then leaving the two organizations. We knew that at that moment Goebbels had had to choose between his heart, which coincided with ours, and his loyalty to Hitler, and he chose the latter. How the Mutschmann incident ended I have no idea. When I entered the Ministry, the head of personnel had apparently not read my CV, no doubt because he never dreamed that OKH would have sent along a lieutenant who had abandoned the Party and SA in 1932.

To return to SA General Marnitz. The same day he joined the NSDAP the flamboyant member introduced himself to Arthur Karl Greiser (1897–1946), NSDAP chargé d'affaires at Danzig. Greiser had not been in the Party much longer than Marnitz, but was also SS, still officially under Röhm, while Himmler only controlled a force of a few hundred. His job was to provide the Fuhrer and other speakers with a bodyguard during meetings. Greiser advised Marnitz to join the SA, although he had already begun, as the head of a Party cell, to achieve the Party quota and was also handling other minor tasks. These were not political jobs as Marnitz had imagined and therefore he took Greiser's advice and volunteered for the SA where he felt – like myself and many others – 'completely at home'.

At the beginning of 1931 when he had been promoted to SA Hauptsturmfuhrer and given charge of his own company at Danzig-Langfuhr, Albert Forster (1902–54), Gauleiter of Danzig, suggested Marnitz should transfer into the SS together with his SA company. He declined; as for most SA men Marnitz felt obliged to contribute towards Hitler's objective that all Germany should become convinced of the goodwill of the Movement. We considered the SA to be an elite, and felt morally superior to the SS, which was practically a corps of bodyguards differing from the police only in being forbidden to bear arms and drawing no salary. This situation was the motive for a rhyme:

> Fear so far, death so near, long live the SA!
> Death so far, always smart, long live the SS!

During the Second World War when the SS represented the best military traditions and had acquired heroic fame as no other fighting unit, in the eyes of friend and foe alike, the leading unit being the *Leibstandarte Adolf Hitler*, nobody remembered this ironic rhyme. An SS commander taught me a verse mocking Röhm after the war. Hitler felt compelled to defend Röhm in his first directive of the year, on 3 February 1931, regretting that he had had to deal with 'reports and statements' against SA leaders particularly regarding 'their private lives'. One such attack was the joke told me by a former SS man who became a cabaret artist postwar: Hung on the wall behind Röhm's desk at the Munich HQ was a neatly framed verse which read:

At five I am going to leave work soon
And ready myself for a happy afternoon.

In the mentioned directive, Hitler wrote: 'The SA is not a college for young ladies, but for tough fighters. The investigation of a man's duties is limited to confirming that SA men and officers are meeting their obligations. Their private lives are only of interest when they conflict with the ethical principles of National Socialism.' As Chancellor, Hitler was right in rejecting Röhm's plans to form a popular militia, This was simply one of the military mind games of the eternal captain. His homosexual inclinations, known to every man and his dog, were not the reason for his being eliminated.* Hitler on the other hand had to prepare with all means available for a war of extermination without compassion, and that as rapidly as possible. That aim could only be achieved based on the principles and example of the Reichswehr. Röhm's ideas therefore had to fail.

---

* In a communiqué from the Reich Press Office during July 1934 it was explained that Röhm's 'unfortunate inclinations' had created such problems as to place the Fuhrer in a 'conflict of conscience'. When the arrests were made, 'the most disgusting activities were discovered'. Some of the SA leaders 'were discovered in bed with young male prostitutes'. The Fuhrer then ordered that this 'pestilence' had to be eradicated forthwith. He was not going to tolerate in future that millions of decent people should be 'burdened or compromised' by sick individuals of this kind'. This dreadful piece of official propaganda was proven to be a lie by *Reichsgesetzblatt*, I 1934, p. 529, which justified retroactively the law 'Gesetz uber Massnahmen der Staatsnotwehr' of 3 July 1934, at Article 1, that the measures taken between 30 June and 2 July 1934 inclusive were lawful to combat acts of treason and high treason, and not homosexuality. See Otto Gritschneider, *Der Fuhrer hat Sie zum Tode verurteilt – Hitlers Röhm-Putsch – Morde vor Gericht*, Munich, 1993, p. 51: quoted in Mario R. Dederichs, *Heydrich*, Munich, 2005, pp. 92–3.

CHAPTER 18

The SA Spirit

On 30 January 1933 the SA was 300,000 strong. What bound these men together before the seizure of power by Adolf Hitler? The historian Bennecke explains it thus: 'The truth is that after the war and the destruction of the National Socialist regime, former SA men, who in 1933 were between twenty and thirty years of age, insisted that the spirit of comradeship they enjoyed was the sign of true *Volksgemeinschaft* [national racial community] which traversed social class, and that this interested them more than the Party programme.* I did not read the programme at that time, and when I flicked through it later, it told me nothing. We practised *Volksgemeinschaft*-life every day in our ranks. One of the main helpers for this book, General von Schmidt, put it this way: 'In the SA community, I learnt with surprise to what point a man is capable of acting with disinterest, demonstrating comradeship and goodwill, and this in an outstanding manner between even the poorest sons of our towns. How many times was I shamed by their example, and morally obliged to pay for the omissions of many years in the face of those simple companions!'

Schmidt explained to me and many other men how destiny had united their hearts. That was the spirit of our old 1933 SA. Today it no longer exists. It succumbed more than half a century ago, together with Germany, destroyed by a world which did not understand it. The SA made many sacrifices to maintain the

---

* Bennecke, *Hitler*.

material and spiritual independence of their country. The figures are these:

Up to 1930:	16 dead, 2,000 injured
1931:	38 dead, 6,000 injured
1932:	78 dead, 10,000 injured
Total	132 dead, 18,000 injured

During the Weimar Republic, 40,000 SA men were prosecuted and received a total of 14,000 years imprisonment and 1.5 million RM in fines. These details were collected by Jean Mabire without giving his sources, in his Röhm biography.* The figures could well be greater. 200 SA deaths were registered up to 30 January 1933 from all causes, and 233 up to 1938 including murders in Austria. The most important SA task before 1933 was the protection of NSDAP meetings and demonstrations. After taking power there was nothing comparable for it to do. Röhm wanted to introduce his impossible ideas, and adopted a position of 'healthy opposition' on the sidelines instead of incorporating the SA into the Third Reich as the Party wanted. Shortly after his death the SA found a suitable role for an organization of millions in pre- and post-military training and in cases of need the teaching of professional trades. Many SA men thought it important to cultivate the spirit of comradeship. This had a knock-on effect for their families and friends, and thus helped create a web across the entire nation.

Historians say that 30 June 1934 marked the beginning of the SA's loss of importance. This is an error because even before that date the SA had no political importance. What attracted attention until mid-1934 was Röhm's lust for power and not so much the power or authority the SA general staff might have had. The interventions at Bad Godesberg, Munich and Berlin did not change its purpose but merely cancelled out the

* Jean Mabire, *Ernst Röhm*, Paris, 1983.

ambitions of a noisy group which lacked power and sought to enlarge SA power in pursuit of a political idea.

When war broke out, and because it went on far longer than had been first thought, the SA began losing its membership to military conscription. Those unfit for the front due to age or other causes were placed with the anti-aircraft service, given work as technicians or served other roles in civil defence. Their leaders clamoured to be sent to the front and put their lives and health at risk as they had done before, during the years of struggle for power. The old SA commanders almost always found death, and died with dignity even at the end of a rope or shot by the victors. One was Hermann Goring, who as SA-Fuhrer had taken part in the march to the Feldherrnhalle in 1923 and suffered a wound which left him in continuous pain only controlled by morphine. When on trial at Nuremberg his old body found the way to do without the morphine and he cheated the hangman with a suicide capsule shortly before he was due to go to the gallows. At age 93 Rudolf Hess, who led the first SA students in Munich, was murdered by strangulation by British agents on 17 August 1987 in the enormous prison at Berlin Spandau after having been incarcerated forty-seven years (four in Britain, three at Nuremberg and forty at Spandau, of which the last twenty were as the solitary occupant of the prison. After his murder, Spandau Prison was demolished.) The youngest SA general, Siegfried Kasche was murdered on 19 June 1947 at Zagreb, Croatia, by Tito's Bolshevists. Other SA leaders lost their lives during and after the capitulation. Schepmann was one of the few to die by natural causes (d. 26 July 1970, aged 76).

Rank Equivalents

Sturmabteilung

SA Mann	Private
Sturmmann	,,
Obersturmmann	,,
Rottenführer	Lance-Corporal
Scharführer	Corporal
Truppführer	Sergeant
Obertruppführer	Staff Sergeant
Haupttruppführer	Company Sergeant-Major
Sturmführer	2nd Lieutenant
Obersturmführer	Lieutenant
Hauptsturmführer	Captain
Sturmbannführer	Major
Obersturmbannführer	Lt Colonel
Standartenführer	Colonel
Oberführer	Major General/Brigadier
Gruppenführer	Lt General
Obergruppenführer	General
Stabschef der SA	SA Chief of Staff
Oberster SA-Führer	Commander in Chief

German Army

Leutnant	2nd Lieutenant
Oberleutnant	Lieutenant
Hauptmann	Captain
Major	Major

Oberstleutnant	Lt Colonel
Oberst	Colonel
Generalmajor	Literal translation is Major General, but equivalent to Brigadier
Generalleutnant	Literal translation is Lt General, but equivalent to Major General
General der Infanterie	General of Infantry (also Cavalry etc), equivalent to Lt General
Generaloberst	Colonel General, equivalent to (full) General

Index